To Kathryn

5.25

QR 3-23-70

DAY

Curriculum Theory

Second Edition

CURRICULUM THEORY

Second Edition

GEORGE A. BEAUCHAMP
Northwestern University

THE KAGG PRESS   Wilmette, Illinois   1968

Library of Congress Catalog Card Number: 68-31038

Printed in the United States of America

Preface

The first serious effort to bring together ideas about curriculum theory was a conference held at the University of Chicago in 1947. Approximately ten years later, it occurred to me that it would be fruitful to examine carefully the status of curriculum theory with particular reference to its dimensions and processes. The examination culminated in the first edition of *Curriculum Theory* in 1961.

Since 1961, a growing number of persons have become interested in curriculum theory, and they have produced a larger volume of literature than ever written before on the subject. There is no doubt in my mind that substantial steps forward have been taken. These circumstances have motivated me to write this second edition of *Curriculum Theory.*

Essentially, the same procedures were followed in the research effort for this book as were followed in preparing the first edition. A fresh look was taken at literature describing practices and concepts relating to theory development in behavioral disciplines related to education for cues leading to a discussion of curriculum theory. Next, cues were sought from efforts in theory development within the broad field of education in the belief that curriculum theory must be a subtheory of educational theory. A third step consisted of noting milestones in the development of ideas about curriculum theory. The results are presented in Chapters 1 through 4. Finally, an analysis was made of the theoretical issues, problems, and alternatives within identified components of curriculum theory. These areas are discussed in Chapters 5 through 9.

I must thank several persons for assistance with this publication. My colleague, Gail M. Inlow, did yoeman duty as critical editor of the manuscript, and I shall be forever in his debt. Wilbur A. Yauch offered many fine suggestions after reading the entire manuscript. Joe Park gave substantial assistance with Chapter 8. Suzanne Beauchamp was both thorough and delightful in final checking of proofs. I am extremely grateful to all of these people and to other colleagues and graduate students who have made helpful criticisms of previous writings. I sincerely thank those authors and publishers who consented to the use herein of materials either paraphrased or directly quoted. Proper credits are given in the text.

My wife, Kathryn, has been an invaluable partner in this entire effort. Only the smallest portion of my gratitude is expressed through dedicating the book to her.

George A. Beauchamp
Evanston, Illinois

TABLE OF CONTENTS

Preface   vii

1. CURRICULUM THEORY AS AN EDUCATIONAL
   PROBLEM   1

   Curriculum Theory in Perspective
   Conceptions in Curriculum Theory

2. THEORY BUILDING   9

   Theory Defined
   Theory Functions
   Characteristics of Theories
   Theorizing Activities
   Summary
   Suggested Readings

3. EDUCATIONAL THEORY   31

   Theory and Practice
   Theory and Philosophy
   Theory in School Administration
   Instructional Theory
   Educational Theory
   Summary
   Suggested Readings

4. DEVELOPMENTS IN CURRICULUM THEORY   55

   Milestones in Curriculum Theory
   Curriculum Theory and Its Ingredients
   Summary
   Suggested Readings

5.   CURRICULUM DESIGN   77

     The Contents of a Curriculum
     Organizing an Instructional Guide
     Trends in Practice
     Summary
     Suggested Readings

6.   CURRICULUM ENGINEERING   108

     Systems of Schooling
     The Curriculum System
     Theoretical Issues
     Summary
     Suggested Readings

7.   CURRICULUM AS A FIELD OF STUDY   145

     Curriculum Textbooks and Courses
     Research
     Common and Uncommon Denominators
     Summary
     Suggested Readings

8.   VALUES IN CURRICULUM THEORY   155

     Value Interpretations
     Values and the Curriculum
     Implications for Curriculum Theory-Building
     Summary
     Suggested Readings

9.   EPILOGUE   171

     Theory Building
     Curriculum Theory Components
     Imponderables

Index   181

Curriculum Theory

Second Edition

1

CURRICULUM THEORY

AS AN

EDUCATIONAL PROBLEM

Education in the United States has developed as a technology rather than as a science. This is to say that most of what we do in schools has come about more from our experience in the practical affairs of running schools than from well-developed scientific theories which would give greater and more systematic meaning to the practices. Schools in our country have been very close to the people. This characteristic is a natural result of demand for mass education with the attendant problems of teacher supply and school construction. Each time in our history that a crisis has confronted public schools, the technology has become more complicated. Whenever a demand for the transmission of an element of our culture to the young has arisen, that element often has become a new school subject. The addition of such subjects as manual training, home economics, modern languages, bio-chemistry, social studies, tool making, and driver education are noteworthy examples. Most of the time these subjects have been added without clear definition of changing roles of the school that demand the new subjects. As a consequence, curriculums of our public schools have grown by the additive process, with social pressures being in large part responsible.

Contrast this procedure with areas of human effort where practices and well-developed theories have a reinforcing relationship. Our scientists and social scientists have developed theories to direct practices and to explain relationships. The theories are modified by technology and research, but they also tend to direct much of the technological development.

In education there has been too little employment of the techniques of science in the development of theories. One reason may be that such an approach appears to many to be impersonal and devoid of values. The products of the scientist tend to be impersonal, but as Conant pointed out, the activities of the scientists are shot through with value judgments.[1] Educators have been concerned with empirical data of all kinds, but they have been unable to make use of the conceptual processes of science in the development of theories. Some explanation may be found in the rapid growth of education in a growing country in which schools have been faced with one crisis after another. Other explanation may be found in lack of ability and interest of educators in theory building work. Explicit rationales for the operations of schools are urgently needed lest chaos be created by diversity in practice. In any case, the day seems to be past when the development of theory in education can continue to ignore the procedures of science.

[1] James B. Conant, *Modern Science and Modern Man* (Garden City, N.Y.: Doubleday and Company, Inc., 1952), p. 107.

CURRICULUM THEORY IN PERSPECTIVE

However, the central theme of this book is not educational theory but curriculum theory. Any educational theory would have to account for all the known components of education including curriculum. Curriculum theory is a sub-theory of educational theory. Furthermore, all theories derive from theories in the established disciplines. This can be illustrated by Figure 1. In essence, it constitutes a theory microcosm of which curriculum theory is a part. At the top of the figure, three basic content categories of theory appear; they consist of the humanities, the natural sciences, and the social sciences. These three categories of theory have the task of explaining and predicting relationships within their respective provinces of knowledge. Emerging from these broad categories of theory are theories in the applied areas of knowledge. These are shown at the second level of the chart, with architecture, engineering, education, law, and medicine used as examples. Theories in the applied areas of knowledge draw their primary authority and information from the basic disciplines. However, it is true that a field such as engineering will draw primarily from the natural sciences, law from the social sciences, and so forth. Each group of theories in the applied areas is undergirded by a series of sub-theories at the third level. The classes of theory presented at the third level are exclusively sub-theories to education. The chart does not include sub-theories for architecture, engineering, law, or medicine. The illustrative sub-theories for education are administrative theories, counseling theories, curriculum theories, instructional theories, and evaluation theories.

Our focus of attention is upon curriculum theories; therefore, in the diagram solid lines have been used to show direct

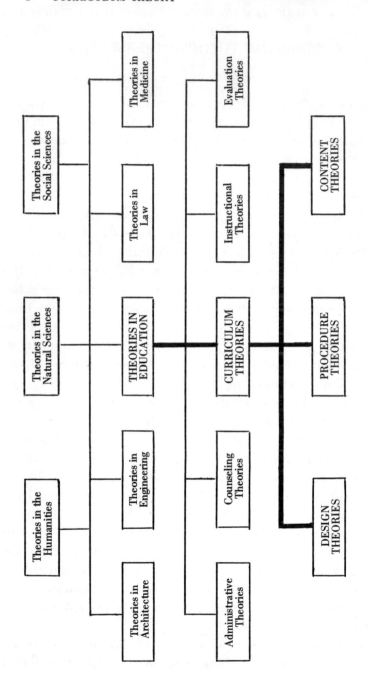

Figure 1. *Curriculum theory in perspective.*

connections between supra- and sub-theories to curriculum. Theories in law or engineering may contribute to administrative theories or curriculum theories, but they are of secondary importance since all of the groups of theories listed at the third level are sub-theories to theories in education. Similarly at the fourth level, design theories, procedure theories, and content theories are illustrative sub-theories of curriculum theories. Administrative theories or instructional theories may influence design theories, but design theories are not sub-theories to them. Again, the chart does not include sub-theories for administrative, counseling, instructional, or evaluation theories. Our main trunk line of concern is indicated by the heavy line from theories in education, to curriculum theories, to the sub-theories of curriculum at the fourth level. What Figure 1 does is show vividly how curriculum theory is an educational problem. Curriculum theory is a necessary link in a series of events which in combination explain education.

CONCEPTS IN CURRICULUM THEORY

The specific dimensions of curriculum theory reside in the concepts and derived generalizations that are unique to the field of curriculum. At least in the very early stages of his work, a theorist must concentrate upon the identification of the most important concepts in his field. In this way, he delimits the subject matter of his field of work. When relationships among concepts are established as generaliaztions, the scientific theorizer begins to form a classification scheme for phenomena within his field. This state of affairs is what Braithwaite referred to as a natural history stage in the development of science.[2] Perhaps this is the stage in which curriculum theory is at the present moment because those who exhibit interest in curriculum are striving to define their basic concepts and to establish relationships among them.

Chief among the problems for the curriculum theorist, however, is the establishment of precise meanings associated with the basic concepts of curriculum. The words have been chosen, but the meanings to be attributed to them are diffused. The important term for curriculum theory is "curriculum." From a theoretical point of view, it is impossible to develop subordinate constructs, or relationships, with other components of education, until ground rules are laid down through meanings ascribed to the basic term "curriculum."

In the opinion of the writer, there are three ways in which the term curriculum is most legitimately used. An individual, for instance, may legitimately speak of *a curriculum.* A curriculum is a written document which may contain many ingredients, but basically it is a plan for the education of pupils during their enrollment in a given school. It is the overall plan that is intended to be used by teachers as a point of departure for developing teaching strategies to be used with specific classroom groups of pupils. A second legitimate use of the term curriculum is to refer to *a curriculum system* as a sub-system of schooling. A curriculum system in schools is the system within which decisions are made about what the curriculum will be and how it will be implemented. A third legitimate use of the term curriculum is to identify *a field of study.* Persons most concerned with curriculum as a field of study are undergraduate and graduate students enrolled in professional education work at colleges

[2]Richard B. Braithwaite, *Scientific Explanation* (New York: Harper and Row, 1960), p. 1.

and universities, professors of curriculum, and curriculum theorists.

There are other interpretations associated with curriculum, but they are difficult to relate to the three so briefly described here. For example, curriculum and instruction frequently are depicted as interchangeable terms. At other times, instruction is conceived to be part of curriculum, or curriculum is thought to be subordinate to instruction. When terms are intermingled in this way, communication is complicated, and it is difficult for anyone to develop research designs that can penetrate the profuse number of variables involved.

With so many uses and interpretations of curriculum as the basic concept in the field, it is easy to imagine the confusion that reigns among subordinate concepts. The problem for organized thinkers in the area is to search out the relationships that need to be established and which will lead to explanatory and predictive generalizations. In the process, operational constructs can be developed that will clarify many of the subordinate concepts within curriculum.

All of these matters constitute the specific dimensions of curriculum theory as an educational problem, and thus they are the subject matter of this entire book. There are really two major parts to the book in addition to the introductory and concluding chapters. The purpose of the first part is to develop a basic rationale for curriculum theorizing beginning with an examination of basic principles of theoretical work in areas related to education, followed by a discussion of theorizing in education, and ending with a discussion of curriculum theory. The first part embraces Chapters 2, 3, and 4. The purpose of the second part is to examine in detail the three ways in which the term curriculum is used and the consequences for the curriculum theorist engaged in the selection and use of concepts inherent in the three uses.

Added to these topics is a chapter devoted to the subject of values as related to curriculum processes and content. The second part embraces Chapter 5 through 8. The final chapter is an attempt to bring things together and to point the way for additional work in curriculum theory.

It is hoped that this treatment of curriculum theory will stimulate two kinds of activity — more precise theory building and more theoretically oriented research. Theory building efforts will help to identify gaps in our knowledge. Theoretically oriented research will help to fill in those gaps. In this way, we can move away from a purely technological operation and toward a behavioral science. Certainly, if there is any hope for developing a discipline of education, sub-theories of education such as curriculum theories will have to be built using the skills and the procedures of the social scientist. It also is hoped that any ideas or procedures herein presented will be checked, challenged, and/or repeated by others who are concerned with the growth of curriculum theory.

2

THEORY BUILDING

If education is to be treated as a science, it must be as an applied behavioral science. As an applied science, education must look to original sources for much of its content and and processes. The same must be said for any sub-divisions of education such as curriculum. If we are to theorize about education, or any sub-division of it, we must look to the work of theoreticians, in related areas. In this case, the related areas are the behavioral sciences.

It is not enough to search among the work of colleagues in the behavioral sciences for models for theories. We must seek for basic understanding in the fundamental processes in theory building. Models may emerge from understanding of the basic processes, or they may grow out of related circumstances. But first, there must be basic understanding.

In this chapter we shall review the use of the concept "theory" and the basic processes associated therewith in literature from behavioral sciences related to education. Parsons gave support to the idea of this kind of search when he indicated: ". . . good general theory in the field of human action, no matter how firmly grounded in one discipline, is inevitably interdisciplinary theory."[1] The review is selective since the objective is to seek direction rather than review exhaustively.

THEORY DEFINED

As one might expect, there is both agreement and disagreement as to the meaning of theory in the disciplines related to education. As stated by Logan and Olmstead:

> Everyone agrees that a theory is, among other things, a set of statements; there is disagreement about what other characteristics any set of statements must have in order to be labeled "theory."[2]

Statements about sets of events differ greatly in complexity. In part, the variation is due to the scope of the series of events. In part, it is due to the degree of sophistication with which the set of events has been treated by theorists in the field of endeavor. In spite of these differences, nearly all serious writers on theory have defined theory in one form or another. Some example definitions of theory will help to illustrate convergent and divergent viewpoints about the meanings associated with theory.

Most definitions of theory express unification of phenomena within the set of events encompassed by the theory. Brodbeck gave us a very forthright notion when she wrote:

[1]Talcott Parsons, "General Theory in Sociology," *Sociology Today*, edited by Robert K. Merton, Leonard Broom, and Leonard S. Cottrell, Jr. (New York: Basic Books, Inc., 1959), p. 37.

[2]Frank Logan and David Olmstead, *Behavior Theory and Social Science* (New Haven: Yale University Press, 1955), p. 4.

Language consists of words and sentences. To the words of ordinary speech correspond the *concepts* of science; to the *sentences* its *definitions,* its *statements of individual fact* and *of laws.* Certain sets of sentences constitute the *theories* of science.[3]

Hall and Lindzey stated that a theory is a set of conventions that "should contain a cluster of relevant assumptions systematically related to each other and a set of empirical definitions."[4] O'Connor noted that in contrasting theory from practice we ". . . refer to a set or system of rules or a collection of precepts which guide or control actions of various kinds."[5] From such definitions one catches the spirit of theory as a unifying phenomenon. The idea of "set" as a homogeneous group seems to be a basic concept in theorizing.

The same idea is expanded when such terms as laws and generalizations are added as the kinds of statement to be ordered into a theory. A definition by Rose illustrates:

> A theory may be defined as an integrated body of definitions, assumptions, and general propositions covering a given subject matter from which a comprehensive and consistent set of specific and testable hypotheses can be deduced logically.[6]

On a somewhat more complicated level, theories are related to laws, hypotheses, and logico-mathematical deduc-

[3]May Brodbeck, "Logic and Scientific Method in Research on Teaching," *Handbook of Research on Teaching,* N.L. Gage, editor (Chicago: Rand McNally and Company, 1963), pp. 44-45.

[4]Calvin S. Hall and Gardner Lindzey, *Theories of Personality* (New York: John Wiley and Sons, Inc., 1957), pp. 10-11.

[5]D. J. O'Connor, *An Introduction to the Philosophy of Education* (London: Routledge and Kegan Paul, 1957), p. 75.

[6]Arnold M. Rose, "Generalizations in the Social Sciences, *American Journal of Sociology,* 59:52, August, 1953.

tions. Abel used these words to voice his interpretation of general theory in the social sciences:

> A general theory is built upon the facts discovered by means of the use of theorems and other conceptual models from empirical data and which have been expressed in the form of laws, correlations, or other types of generalizations. It involves synthesis and is directed to the formulation of propositions about universals.[7]

Feigl's frequently quoted definition is in a similar vein, but it is more detailed.

> I purpose to define a "theory" as a set of assumptions from which can be derived by purely logico-mathematical procedures, a larger set of empirical laws. The theory thereby furnishes an explanation of these empirical laws and unifies the originally relatively heterogeneous areas of subject matter characterized by those empirical laws. Even though it must be admitted that there is no sharp line of demarcation (except a purely arbitrary one) between theoretical assumptions and empirical laws, the distinction, at least in the sense of gradation, is illuminating from a methodological point of view.[8]

In addition to the two dimensions of unification and universal propositions, a third needs to be added to complete the characterization of theory definitions, and that is the dimension of prediction. Some theorists choose to define theory so that prediction is the key dimension. For example, Travers noted: "A theory as developed by a scientist is . . . a set of generalizations believed to have some value in predicting important events."[9] Actually, full definition of theory satisfies all of these characteristics. Kerlinger combined all of the dimensions that have been mentioned when he wrote

[7]Theodore Abel, "The Present Status of Social Theory," *American Sociological Review*, 17:162, April, 1952.

[8]Herbert Feigl, "Principles and Problems of Theory Construction in Psychology," *Current Trends in Psychological Theory* (Pittsburgh: University of Pittsburgh Press, 1951), p. 182.

[9]Robert M. W. Travers, *An Introduction to Educational Research* (second edition; New York: The Macmillan Company, 1964), p. 16.

the following:

> *A theory is a set of interrelated constructs (concepts), definitions, and propositions that presents a systematic view of phenomena by specifying relations among variables, with the purpose of explaining and predicting the phenomena.*[10]

THEORY FUNCTIONS

Our understanding of the meaning of theory may be augmented if we note some of the functions associated with theory. The range of these is very broad, but at the same time they lack cohesiveness. Theorists may exhibit different focal points for their efforts, but at the same time there is general agreement among scientists and philosophers of science that ". . . theories fulfill the three functions of, (1) description, (2) prediction, and (3) explanation."[11] These functions bear upon the theory that the scientist tries to understand, and they have implications for persons who may be using theories. Gowan acknowledged the latter when he said:

> But turn theory around and point it toward the person using the theory. A different set of functions seems to be prominent when we look at the theorist at work in research. Here the theory helps the researcher to *analyze* data, to make a short-hand summarization or *synopsis* of data and relations, and to *suggest* new things to try out. Theory functions in analysis, in synopsis, in power of suggestion or speculation. Theory functions as something to think with, to help in one's work.[12]

[10]Fred N. Kerlinger, *Foundations of Behavioral Research* (New York: Holt, Rinehart and Winston, Inc., 1965), p. 11.

[11]O'Connor, *op. cit.*, 81.

[12]D. B. Gowin, "Can Educational Theory Guide Practice?" *Educational Theory*, 13:8, January, 1963.

Probably the most simple function of a theory is to provide a system for classifying the knowledge of that theoretical field. Homans has expressed this function in the following picturesque way:

> Even the most fragile theory has its uses. In its lowest form, as a classification, it provides a set of pigeonholes, a filing cabinet, in which fact can accumulate . . . . In time the accumulation makes necessary a more economical filing system, with more cross references, and a new theory is born.[13]

The ordering of facts and observations into some scheme is fundamental to description of any field about which theorizing is to be done. It is a way of arranging information so that the scope and the internal relationships of the total body of information is more visible. As Brodbeck stated: "A theory not only explains and predicts, it also unifies phenomena."[14]

At a higher level, are added those functions that permit moving beyond classification or collection of facts to action of broader scope such as that involved in deduction or prediction. Whereas it is true that the ordering of information in a systematic manner is a task of theorizing, the task really is but a prelude to the fulfillment of the larger functions of theory. With these being description, prediction, and explanation, theory building reaches its most systematic level when the resulting theory becomes a full-blown logico-deductive system, or a logico-mathematical system. These high-level goals are reached most easily in the natural sciences, but in the social sciences the complications of the sets

[13]George Homans, *The Human Group* (New York: Harcourt, Brace, and World, Inc., 1950), p. 5.

[14]*Op. cit.*, p. 70.

of events to be explained by theories may force theorists to temporarily lesser levels of achievement. Very few theoretical systems utilizing symbols and mathematical structures have been created in the social sciences. Instead, verbal models are used extensively as ways of representing particular phenomena. Nevertheless, theories in the social sciences must meet the basic criteria for theorizing and these include the organization of relationships so that they are better explained and so that predictions can be made for events not yet observed from known relationships.

We return for a moment to Kerlinger's definition which illustrates the three theory functions of description, prediction, and explanation. First the definition calls for description through the character of the propositions offered and the delineated relationships among the propositions and constructs. By studying what variables are related and how they are related, the researcher is able to develop predictable relationships between certain variables. All of these explain the set of events.

It has been emphasized that a main purpose of theories is to explain selected phenomena or events. The idea of explanation is interpretable two ways. One is to give an account of something; the other is to account for something.[15] This distinction is an interesting one because it relates to the levels of theorizing described in the foregoing paragraphs. Very often those who become involved in classification as a theorizing activity are working at the task of giving an account of something; whereas, the individual who builds a predictive system is accounting for something through the established predictable relationships. It is one thing to give an anecdotal account of the daily behavior of an aggressive child in a

[15]This distinction was made by Herbert Feigl in a speech given at a colloquium at Northwestern University in January 1966. Feigl holds that the latter is the task of theory.

school classroom, but another to relate that meaningfully to the phenomenon of prediction.

CHARACTERISTICS OF THEORIES

We can further expand our understanding of the processes of theorizing by examining more carefully the characteristics, or ingredients, of theories. We look first at the kinds of terms and statements used conventionally by theorists to express explanations of sets of events.

Terms

A crucial aspect of a scientist's work is his use of technical terms. He is obligated, as a scientist, to carefully define his terms and to use them consistently thereafter in his work. Such consistency is particularly relevant in theorizing. There are various ways of designating the classes of terms used in theory work. Selected examples, the following by Brodbeck as one, should help to illustrate the point:

> A theory contains two classes of descriptive terms: basic or "primitive," and defined. The basic terms of a theory are those that are not themselves defined within the theory, but all other descriptive terms of the theory are defined by means of them. The basic terms of a theory must occur in its axioms and may also re-occur in its theorems. Its defined terms occur only in the theorems.[16]

Under the subject of "theoretical terms," Kaplan specified observation terms, indirect observable terms, constructs, and theoretical terms. However, he indicated little consistency in

[16]*Op. cit.*, p. 70.

use of this nomenclature and ended his discussion by noting that there really are no differences among the discriminations.[17] Gordon and others divided theory terms into three main classes: primitive terms, key terms, and theoretical terms.[18]

Despite the various ways of designating classes of terms, the theorist probably should be aware of at least three classes he might be called upon to choose and use. First, there are those terms that are used in science and in general language in common. These are the words that make the sentences of a theory such as many of the verbs and adjectives. It is not necessary that they be defined at all, much less operationally defined, because their use has become commonly accepted. A second group consists of those concepts that are basic to the set of events being explained. These are well-defined constructs, and they usually are operationally defined. Such terms as "molecule" in chemistry, "mass" in physics, or "curriculum" in education would fit in this category. A third group consists of those that are essential to the theory. These words have meaning for the system of events being encompassed by the theory, but they cannot be identified by direct observation. Such terms as "emotional need," "persecution complex," or "attitude" belong in this category.

Statements

A theory, by definition, contains a set of statements within which the terms are used. The statements themselves fall into different classes just as the terms do. Statements are referred to differentially as facts, definitions, proposi-

[17]Abraham Kaplan, *The Conduct of Inquiry* (San Francisco: Chandler Publishing Company, 1964), pp. 54-60.

[18]Ira J. Gordon, Chairman, "Theories of Instruction: A Set of Guidelines," a position paper prepared by the Commission on Instructional Theory and presented at the Annual Conference of the Association for Supervision and Curriculum Development, NEA at Dallas, Texas in March, 1967.

tions, postulates, hypotheses, deductions, assumptions generalizations, laws, axioms, theorems, and so forth. Sometimes these referents are used interchangeably and in slightly varying contexts.

It helps curriculum theorists to look at theory statements in the light of the functions expected of theories. The primary ones in this connection are explanation and prediction. The statements employed to formulate theories must fulfill those functions. In the words of Brodbeck ". . . the scientist looks for laws or connections among facts in order to explain and predict phenomena."[19] It is very important for the theorist to keep in mind that he must be concerned with relationships, or connections, among the phenomena under his consideration. This is what distinguishes in great part his work from that of the scientist who is solely concerned with the discovery of fact. The theorist must explain his set of events whether he knows about all of the elements of that set of events or not. This is illustrated in Figure 2. In Figure 2, A, B, and C are subsets of the universal set ABC. ABC represents the set of events to be explained by a theory. Subset A represents those events of known dimensions, which might be expressed as statements of fact, law, or principle. Subset B represents those events of assumed dimensions, which might be expressed as assumptions, propositions, postulates, or in some other way to reflect tentative information that does not reach the pinnacle of certainty exemplified by fact or law. Subset C represents those events that are part of the universal, or total, set of events for which adequate explanation is not yet available.

It could be said that in his drive to describe, explain, and predict the theorist is striving to work himself out of business, for he is constantly deriving new laws and seeking new relationships among the laws expressed by the theory. One

[19]*Op. cit.*, p. 67.

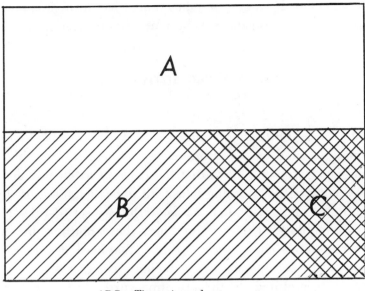

ABC = The universal set
A = Events of known dimensions
B = Events of assumed dimensions
C = Events of unknown dimensions

Figure 2. A set of events constituting a theory.

might think that within a given set of events all of the laws and their interrelationships could be stated and the theory itself thereby become a higher law. However, the theorist is never satisfied with that condition if it ever occurs. He then seeks out new relationships by combining sets of events into a new universal set and then proceeding with the search for new relationships and new laws in a new theory. Kaplan expressed this heuristic function of theory when he stated: "What is important is that laws propagate when they are united in a theory: theory serves as matchmaker, midwife, and godfather all in one."[20] The great advances in the sci-

[20]Op. cit., p. 303.

ences are made by theory building more than through empiricism because of this generative function of theorizing.

THEORIZING ACTIVITIES

More insight into theory and its processes is possible by examining selected tasks performed by the theorist. Two things stand out glaringly. One is that the range of activity is large. The second is that working rules tend to be dictated more by the choice of activity than by any arbitrary set of rules for theory building. These points may be amplified by an examination of some of the suggestions that have been made.

The language used in theory building is a matter of concern as exemplified by the attention currently being given to discovery and delineation of concepts and to the problems of definition of terms. For example, Homans listed the following rules for theory builders, most of which have to do with problems of communicating:

> Look first at the obvious, the familiar, the common. In a science that has not established its foundations, these are the things that best repay study.
>
> State the obvious in its full generality. Science is an economy of thought only if its hypotheses sum up in a simple form a large number of facts.
>
> Talk about one thing at a time. That is, in choosing your words, (or more pedantically, concepts) see that they refer not to several classes of fact at the same time but to one and to one only. Corollary: Once you have chosen your words, always use the same words when referring to the same thing.
>
> Cut down as far as you dare the number of things you are talking about. "As few as you may; as many as you must," is the rule governing the number of classes of fact you take into account.

Once you have started to talk, do not stop until you have finished. That is, describe systematically the relationships between the facts designated by your words.

Recognize that your analysis must be abstract, because it deals with only a few elements of the concrete situation. Admit the dangers of abstraction, especially when action is required, but do not be afraid of abstraction.[21]

Mouly identified the following four characteristics of a good theory which have implications for theory building activities:

1. A theoretical system must permit interpretations, and deductions which can be tested empirically — that is, it must provide the means for its own interpretation and verification.

2. Theory must be compatible both with observation and with previously validated theories.

3. Theories must be stated in simple terms; that theory is best which explains the most in the simplest form.

4. Scientific theories must be based on empirical facts and relationships.[22]

More specifically, curriculum theorists need to think in terms of the precise activities they perform when working at theorizing. One such activity is the formulation of definitions. A second is the classification of relevant information into homogeneous categories. A third, and very important one, is the making of inferences and predictions and the testing of them in the crucible of research. A fourth is the development of models. A fifth is sub-theory formation. All five of these principal theory-building activities are crucial; therefore, each of them will be discussed more fully in the following pages.

[21]*Op. cit.*, pp. 6-17.

[22]George J. Mouly, *The Science of Educational Research* (New York: American Book Company, 1963), p. 58.

Definition of Terms

Description of theory, rules laid down by Homans, and the characteristics described by Mouly, all carry the emphatic message that careful definition of terms is an essential ingredient in the work of a theorist. Two rules seem to govern the activity of definition. One is clarity of wording to assure exact meaning; the other is consistency in use of terms once they have been defined. The terms or constructs of any area of scientific endeavor are the subject matter of that area. The technical terms or constructs of physics and biology, for instance, distinguish between the two sciences. They are the tools for thinking and communicating.

If the reader were to review any significant portion of the literature discussing kinds of definitions and rules for making them, he would find a plethora of names attributed to different kinds of definitions and different kinds of terms or concepts. The terms that the theorist is most likely to be concerned with are general terms, basic concepts, and theoretical terms. For purposes of establishing definition, the theorist would be concerned primarily with the basic and theoretical terms. Brodbeck distinguished between nominal and operational definitions.[23] Nominal definitions give the attributes associated with the term or concept. In this way a term is explained by listing the boundaries of interpretation. Operational definitions, on the other hand, are more complicated in that the conditions under which a concept is used are a part of the definition. The operational definition assumes an "if—then" condition meaning that if certain conditions exist, then the statement within which the term is used is true. Or, a term is recognized if prescribed conditions exist. When a term is a theoretical term, the concept usually is called an operational construct.

[23]*Op. cit.*, pp. 48-51.

There seems to be universal agreement that definition of technical terms is an important and a critical activity for the theorist. Two reasons predominate. The selection and definition of terms or concepts aid in defining the subject matter boundaries for the theorist's work, and the consistent use of the defined terms improves explanation and prediction.

Classification

Classification is another theory building activity. It is reiterated here that Homans referred to classification as the lowest form of theory, but he pointed out the possibility of a classification system becoming or producing new theory. Classification, however, need not always be thought of as a simple pigeonholing activity. Hall and Lindzey pointed out that one of the functions of a theory is to incorporate known findings into a consistent and reasonable framework.[24] In this sense, classification as a theory-building activity becomes a means of organizing and integrating what is known about the areas in which the theorizing activity is being conducted. Through classification, it is possible for the classifier to become aware of the voids in knowledge necessary to give meaning to a given activity or series of events. It is the function of research to fill these gaps. The observation of relationships among classified elements can be included as part of the classification activity.

Sometimes a developed classification scheme, or a taxonomy, actually is called a theory. Such designation is often misleading because a classification scheme cannot fulfill all of the requisites of a theory. Classification as a theorizing activity helps to group facts and generalizations into homogeneous groups, but it does not explain the interrelationships

[24]Hall and Lindzey, *op. cit.*, pp. 13-14.

among the groups or the relationships among the facts and generalizations within any single group. In a sense, developing a classification scheme is a terminal activity. A theory, on the other hand, fosters new relationships and conditions for understanding. Nonetheless, the development of classification schemes is a theorizing activity.

Inference, Prediction, Research

There is a complex of theory building activities that we shall include under the term inference. In general, they consist of acts that go beyond the known or the observed. One of these is the making of assumptions. A theorist may wish to assume relationships to exist; he may assume cause and effect relationships, or he may assume pertinence of additional fact. He may make any of these assumptions for purposes of establishing continuity or meaning in his theory, or he may make them for operational purposes in research.

The use of the hypothesis in theory building is as clear as it is in research. One uses the hypothesis as a tool for verifying or rejecting a stated assumption. From repeated use of the hypothesis, the theory builder can formulate postulates, theorems, or laws governing the interrelationships of his theory elements.

Two additional terms related to the general process of inference are generalization and deduction. A theorist may generalize from a group of related or similar observations of events. A series of generalizations may lead him to form deductions about his observations which may, in turn, lead him to hypotheses to be tested. Or he may generalize from deduced hypotheses which have been tested and verified

There is no question but that some of the aforementioned terms included here under the concept of inference are used interchangeably or synonymously in the literature. They reveal the variety of processes that the theory builder has at his command to do his work. The main point of inference as a theory building activity is that one must go beyond the simple observation and classification of observations if a working theory is to be built.

It is stated repeatedly in the literature that the real test of a theory is the reliability of the prediction that can be made from it. The principal function of a theory is to give greater meaning to a set of events; the greater meaning would involve both what is known about the set of events from observations already made and the unknown expressed through inference of some sort. Whenever a set of events is perpetuated, the existence of theory gives greater meaning to the practice of the events because a rationale exists for the events in spite of the unknown. In learning theory, for example, the phenomenon of transfer of training must be accounted for to explain certain kinds of learning behavior. Both facts and inference must be posed by the learning theorist before transfer of training can become a useful concept in his theory. But the real test of the theorist's structure of the transfer of training concept comes when transfer effect is predicted by means of the theory in a behavioral situation, and the prediction is subsequently tested.

The struggle for prediction in theory was uniquely expressed by Bales:

> As a predictor, the scientific theorizer, like the practical human being he is theorizing about, has to reduce his demands for an omniscient information-gathering apparatus if he wants to predict forward in real time from real information. The trick in improving prediction, since omniscience is so hard to come by, must lie in learning how to get more information or how to make more and better inferences from what we have, or both, and to do either or both before something else happens. These are the requirements of naturalistic prediction, and all good theory must eventually face up to them. But as a theorizer, the scientific

predictor, like the theorizing human being he is predicting about, has to be prepared to think and talk about states of affairs to which he has had no empirical access, as he struggles by symbolic means to construct an omniscient perspective.[25]

Inference, prediction, and research are the activities that really distinguish the work of the theorist. They result in the creating of laws and the identifying of relationships among the laws. Implied in these processes is a movement from hunch, or assumption, to generalization based on some evidence (postulates), to deductions from the postulates, to hypotheses to be researched for purposes of stating laws that improve explanation of the set of events. The quality of theorizing is a function of the precision with which the theorist uses these processes.

Use of Models

Models are analogies. They are a way of representing given phenomena, but they are not the phenomena. A model of an ocean liner is not the actual ship. A set of blueprints is not a house. A diagram of the intersection of two functional spaces is not the set of events giving rise to the diagram. Functionally, models are used to represent events and event interactions in a highly compact and illustrative manner. So employed, they help to explain facts or events that are puzzling. Specifically, they are an aid in theory building.

Kaplan distinguished five different meanings associated with the term "model." One is any theory presented with a degree of mathematical precision. A second is a semantic model analogous to some subject-matter. A third is a physical model. A fourth is a formal model, a model of a theory. And

[25]Robert F. Bales, "Small-Group Theory Research," *Sociology Today*, edited by Robert K. Merton, Leonard Broom, and Leonard S. Cottrell, Jr. (New York: Basic Books, Inc., 1959), p. 297.

a fifth is an interpretive model for a formal theory.[26] Brodbeck claimed two major uses of the term. On the one hand, a model she said, is used for highly speculative or quantified theories. On the other hand, the set of laws for one theory can be used as a model for another when the laws of the two are of the same form or isomorphic.[27] In spite of the labels put on various forms or kinds of models, they basically are either replicas of a set of laws or events, or they represent the set of laws or events symbolically A good point was made by O'Connor when he wrote:

> Thus models in science act like metaphors in language; they enlighten us by suggesting arguments by analogy from known resemblances to resemblances so far unnoticed. They may also act as aids to the type of explanation discussed below. But by themselves, they are no more than a useful stimulus to the process of explanation.[28]

In theorizing, models can serve several functions. Fattu depicted them as providing ways of representation, rules of inference, interpretation, and visualization.[29] Models are useful tools, and theorists make extensive use of them. Like the classification scheme, however, the model is not the theory. The person developing a theory cannot be satisfied with modeling except as a means to an end.

Sub-theory Formation

One of the things that characterizes a mature and compre-

[26]*Op. cit.*, pp. 267-268.

[27]*Op. cit.*, pp. 88-93.

[28]*Op. cit.*, p. 90.

[29]N. A. Fattu, "A Model of Teaching as Problem Solving," *Theories of Instruction*, edited by James B. Macdonald and Robert R. Leeper (Washington: the Association for Supervision and Curriculum Development, NEA, 1965), pp. 63-64.

hensive theory is the development of sub-theories. Sub-theories tend to broaden the scope of a theory as well as to improve the total explanation of the sets of events involved. However, one should not confuse the development of competing theories in a given area with the development of sub-theories in any one theory. For example, it is one thing to talk about the development of learning theories in psychology such as those of Thorndike, Hull, Tolman, or Lewin. It is quite another for any single theory to be distinguished by its unique sub-theories in regard to such issues as transfer, motivation, verbal learning, or retention.

SUMMARY

The purpose of this chapter was to present the meaning and consequences of theory building. The following paragraphs seem to be warranted conclusions.

Theory is defined in several ways. There is general agreement that a theory is a set of statements explaining some series of events. Variations in definition are due to the character of the statement and the kind of event relevant to the theory.

The primary functions of theories are description, prediction, and explanation. These functions are both demanding upon and of service to the theorist. They demand the vigor of description and explanation, and at the same time, they serve as a directive force for the theorist's work.

A theory is composed of a set of statements. Essential to the statements are the terms that define the subject matter of the area. In addition to the commonly used terms that have accepted meanings, there are the terms that are basic to the set of events being explained and the essential theoretical terms. Statements of a theory within which the terms are used may be expressed in such forms as statements of fact, definitions, propositions, postulates, hypotheses, deductions, assumptions, generalizations, laws, axioms, or theorems.

The processes of theorizing can be pinpointed further by identifying some of the tasks for people concerned with theory building. As in all scientific work, the careful definition of technical terms and constructs is one important task. Another is the classification of known and assumed information. Probably the most critical and unique tasks in theorizing are the making and testing of inferences and predictions. Two additional activities are the development of models and sub-theories.

The work of the theorist is broad in scope and intensity. Few people will perform at all possible levels. The uninitiated may begin with some limited task, but it is predictable that his work will broaden at every turn.

SUGGESTED READINGS

Abel, Theodore, "The Present Status of Social Theory," *American Sociological Review*, 17:156-167, April, 1952.

Bales, Robert F. "Small-Group Theory and Research," *Sociology Today*. Robert K. Merton, Leonard Broom, and Leonard S. Cottrell, Jr. editors. New York: Basic Books, Inc., 1959, pp. 293-305.

Braithwaite, Richard B. *Scientific Explanation*. New York: Harper and Row, 1960.

Brodbeck, May. "Logic and Scientific Method in Research on Teaching," *Handbook of Research on Teaching*, N.L. Gage, editor. Chicago:Rand McNally and Company, 1963, pp. 44-93.

Brodbeck, May. "Models, Meaning, and Theories," *Symposium on Sociological Theory*, Llewellyn Gross, editor. Evanston: Row Peterson and Company, 1959, pp. 373-403.

Conant, James B. *Modern Science and Modern Man*. Garden City, N.Y.: Doubleday and Company, Inc., 1952.

Feigl, Herbert. "Principles and Problems of Theory Construction in Psychology," *Current Trends in Psychological Theory*. Pittsburgh: University of Pittsburgh Press, 1951, pp. 179-213.

Gowin, D. B. "Can Educational Theory Guide Practice?" *Educational Theory*, 13:6-12, January, 1963.

Hall, Calvin S. and Gardner Lindzey. *Theories of Personality.* New York: John Wiley and Sons, Inc., 1957.

Homans, George. *The Human Group.*New York: Harcourt, Brace and World, Inc., 1950.

Kaplan, Abraham. *The Conduct of Inquiry.* San Francisco: Chandler Publishing Company, 1964.

Kerlinger, Fred N. *Foundations of Behavioral Research.* New York: Holt, Rinehart, and Winston, Inc., 1965.

Logan, Frank and David Olmstead. *Behavior Theory and Social Science.* New Haven: Yale University Press. 1955.

Marx, Melvin H. (ed.).*Theories in Contempory Psychology*. New York: The Macmillan Company, 1963.

Miller, James G. "Toward A General Theory for Behavioral Sciences," *American Psychologist*, 10:513-531. 1955.

Mouly, George J. *The Science of Educational Research.* New York: American Book Company, 1963.

O'Connor, D. J. *An Introduction to the Philosophy of   Education.* Routledge and Kegan Paul, 1957.

Parsons, Talcott and Edward A. Shils (eds.). *Foundations of Modern Sociological Theory.* Glenco, Ill.: The Free Press, 1961.

Parsons, Talcott, "General Theory in Sociology," *Sociology Today*. Robert K. Merton, Leonard Broom, and Leonard S. Cottrell, Jr., editors. New York: Basic Books, Inc., 1959, pp. 3-38.

Prior, Moody E. *Science and the Humanities.* Evanston: Northwestern University Press. 1962.

Rose, Arnold M. "Generalizations in the Social Sciences," *American Journal of Sociology*, 59:49-58, July, 1953.

Rose, Arnold M. *Theory and Method in the Social Sciences.* Minneapolis: University of Minnesota Press, 1954.

Spears, William D. "Learning Theory and Objective Psychology in Education," *Educational Theory*, 10:107-119, April, 1960.

Toulmin, Stephen. *The Philosophy of Science.* New York: Harper and Row, 1960.

Travers, Robert M. W. *An Introduction to Educational Research.* Second edition. New York: The Macmillan Company, 1964.

3

EDUCATIONAL THEORY

Against this background of general information about the processes of theorizing, we turn now to an examination of the kinds of theorizing done within the broad field of education. Obviously, it is beyond the scope of this writing to review the entire history of the use of the concept "theory" in education or to review the nature of all so-called educational theories. We can, and do, however, relate the meaning and use of theory in related disciplines to its meaning and use in education.

Traditionally, the word "theory" has been employed in educational literature without definition. For example, in the otherwise carefully prepared publication, the *Encyclopedia of Educational Research,* neither "theory nor ' aducational theory" was indexed much less defined. There are two possible explanations for the omission. One is that the dimensions of educational theory had not been defined carefully enough for the topics to be discussed in an orderly fashion. A second is that there was not sufficient research on the subject to warrant its treatment in an encyclopedia devoted exclusively to research. In discussing the status of educational theory as of 1959, Bayles claimed that educational theory in the United States seemed to be in "a state of suspended animation." In his opinion, assumptions about the social context of education need to be clarified before a sound theoretical structure can be built.[1] About the same time, Travers labeled the theories used in educational research as generalizations, but generalizations without the certainty, usefulness, or status of law.[2] These are illustrations of the failure of scholars in education to introduce the rigors of scientific theorizing to the sets of events attributable to the field of education.

Despite these apparent shortcomings, theory in education has been a topic of serious discussion for a number of years, and in recent ones, the procedures of the natural and social scientist applied to the description and explanation of educational phenomena has opened up new vistas. A reasonable prediction is that educational theory will grow, but it will grow first from the sub-theories now being developed within the broad field of education. A review of the literature treating educational theory reveals that the subject is discussed under the following general headings: theory and practice, theory and philosophy, theory in school administration, instructional theory, and complete educational theory.

THEORY AND PRACTICE

Educational literature contains abundant discourse on the

[1]Ernest Bayles, "Present Status of Educational Theory in the U. S." *School and Society*, 87:5-7, January, 1959.

[2]Robert M. W. Travers, *An Introduction to Educational Research* (New York: The Macmillan Company, 1958), p. 19.

subject of the relationships between theory and practice. Unfortunately, most of it takes a negative instead of a constructive approach. The point of view is that theory is something to be tolerated in small quantities at the college or university level, but to be forgotten or downgraded by classroom teachers, who are expected to be "practical" people. To elaborate this point of view any further would be a waste of the reader's time. The literature in support of it is not based upon a careful consideration of the relationships that need to exist between theory and practice if either is to be consistent and constructive. No doubt, part of the problem is failure of persons espousing this point of view to define the key terms employed, especially the term "theory."

To some extent, confusion is multiplied by failure of commentators to discriminate between research that contributes to the formation of laws pertaining to explanation and prediction, and research applied to field situations which are not necessarily related to any larger series of events. Theory by its very nature is impractical. The world of practicality is built around clusters of specific events. The world of theory derives from generalizations, laws, axioms, and theorms explaining specific events and the relationships among them.

The fact that the worlds of theory and practice are different does not minimize the known interrelationships that exist between them. The operational vistas opened up and explained by theories increase the possible choices of behaving for the practitioner; the theories however, do not tell him how to act. A theory may clarify relationships among any given set of events, but it does not and cannot direct the execution of that set of events. Newsome made this distinction clear when he noted that theory is not what is practiced[3]

[3]George L. Newsome, Jr., "In What Sense Is Theory a Guide to Practice in Education?" *Educational Theory*, 14:36, January, 1964.

A person cannot practice a set of logically related statements; he performs an activity. Theories of instruction, for example, might account for classroom discipline, grouping practices, lesson planning, and instructional materials as components of instruction, but the theories cannot tell teachers how to behave with respect to those functions. Conversely, empirical information may be accumulated as a result of practices in schooling, but the accumulated data will not in itself explain or predict similar events elsewhere. Nevertheless, as Gowin put it, " . . . it is the job of educational theory to guide educational practices."[4] In turn, theory is modified by practice and research that emanates from it.

THEORY AND PHILOSOPHY

It is to be expected that educational literature reveals a very close relationship between educational philosophy and educational theory. In this connection, there are two kinds of theory — prescriptive theory and descriptive theory. Prescriptive theory is related primarily to philosophy; descriptive theory is related primarily to science.

The closeness of the provinces of philosophy and theory was illustrated by Dewey in the statement:

> If we are willing to conceive education as the process of forming fundamental dispositions, intellectual and emotional, toward nature and fellow men, philosophy may even be defined *as the general theory of education.*[5]

[4]D. B. Gowin, "Can Educational Theory Guide Practice?" *Educational Theory*, 13:8, January, 1963.

[5]John Dewey, *Democracy and Education* (New York: The Macmillan Company, 1916), p. 383.

If one accepts the above conclusion, it becomes obvious that many theories must be developed within the general area of philosophy to account for the many dimensions of education and for differing basic philosophies. For example, a good philosophy must encompass a theory of knowledge. A philosophy of education comparably should lead to the formulation of a theory of method. Values and ethics, both in the purview of philosophy, play a significant role in education. That philosophy has a close relationship to theory development is thus self-evident.

Various philosophies of education have been posed as theories of education. In an issue of *School and Society* devoted to educational theories, several different theories based upon philosophical positions were analyzed. Broudy expoused the the cause of realism.[6] Butler defended modern idealism.[7] McMurray identified and elaborated the status of pragmatism in education.[8] Brameld, as would be expected, went to the defense of reconstructionism.[9] Each of these positions is dictated by philosophical attitudes toward the role of the school, the nature of knowledge, the nature and derivation of values, and the nature of man. All of these latter impinge on the education function.

In analyzing confusion and conflict in educational theory, Black labeled four theories: Traditionalist, Progressive, the Learning-Product Theory, and the Learning-Process Theory. The Traditionalist adherents were identified with the transmission of the cultural heritage as the role of the school in

[6]Harry S. Broudy, "Realism in American Education," *School and Society*, 87:11-14, January 17, 1959.

[7]J. Donald Butler, "Idealism in Education Today," *School and Society*, 87: 8-10, January 17, 1959.

[8]Foster McMurray, "The Present Status of Pragmatism in Education," *School and Society*, 87:14-18, January 17, 1959.

[9]Theodore Brameld, "Imperatives for a Reconstructed Philosophy of Education," *School and Society*, 87:18-20, January 17, 1959.

the manner of the pre-Rousseau period. The Progressive adherents were identified as being primarily concerned with the growth of the individual, a late nineteenth-century phenomenon. The Learning-Product adherents looked to such persons as Herbart, Judd, Morrison, and F. W. Parker for a point of view. The emphasis was on transmission of the social heritage which took the individual into account. The Learning-Process adherents were associated with such persons as Rousseau, Petalozzi, Frobel, William James, G. Stanley Hall, John Dewey, Kilpatrick, Childs, Bode, and Harold Rugg. They emphasized the individual but recognized the school's role in the transmission of cultural heritage.[10] In 1966, Black restated his viewpoints on the same subject. Again he placed in polar positions Extreme Progressivism and Extreme Traditionalism with Learning-Process Theory and the Learning-Product Theory interposed between them. He stated:

> This four-fold classificatory scheme thus recognizes four aspects of education and distinguishes the four classes of educational theories according to differences in emphasis. Four concepts — education as transmission of the social heritage, education as individual development, education as a product, and education as a process — are the differentiating factors.[11]

Black concluded by averring that present-day philosophers lean toward the positions they espouse because of their commitment to specific philosophies such as Idealism, Realism, or Pragmatism.

In this kind of classification of positions, more is taken into account than philosophy. Some of the associations are dependent upon acceptance of findings in psychology, particularly learning and child development. Nevertheless, there is

[10]Hugh C. Black, "Confusion and Conflict in Educational Theory: an Analysis," *Peabody Journal of Education*, 30:153-160, November, 1952.

[11]Hugh C. Black, "A Four-fold Classification of Educational Theories," *Educational Theory*, 16:289, July, 1966.

a great deal of reciprocal conversation about educational philosophy and educational theory even to the extent of using the two terms as synonyms.

THEORY IN SCHOOL ADMINISTRATION

One special interest group in education, professors of school administration, are currently giving serious attention to the problem of theorizing. What they actually have been doing is building a sub-theory of educational theory, namely the theory of administration. Much of their effort has been sponsored by the University Council for Educational Administration, the National Conference for Professors of Educational Administration, and the Cooperative Program in Educational Administration. Individuals working on these projects have been concerned primarily with the improvement of the administration of the nations's schools and the teaching of school administration in colleges and universities, but they have used theory development as their route to improvement.

A characteristic feature of these attempts has been the insistence that education utilize the theoretical contributions of disciplines related to education, particularly those of the social sciences, for purposes of theory building in administraion. Theorists in school administration have been following the same kinds of rules for theoretical work that were indicated in Chapter 2. Their efforts, for the most part, are of recent vintage. An early written expression of their organized effort was the signal monograph by Coladarci and Getzels in 1955.[12] Among the most recent is the book by Halpin

[12]Arthur P. Coladarci and Jacob Getzels, *The Use of Theory in Educational Administration* (Stanford: School of Education, 1955).

in 1966.[13] It is not necessary for us to review the details of these efforts here. We make note, however, of some of the uses made of fundamental theorizing procedures.

For one, the theorists in administration have employed the meanings of theory and theorizing in the accepted traditions of the other behavioral sciences. Most writers on administrative theory, make use of Feigl's definition of theory, or they create a derivative from it. For example, Coladarci and Getzels recognized the predictive functions of theory when they pointed out that:

> The term "theory" is often used to mean general principles which seem to predict or account for events with an accuracy so much better than chance that we may say that the principles are "true."[14]

In discussing the construction of theories, Halpin identified the basic elements of a theory as follows:

> Theories cannot be produced on demand: they evolve, and they evolve in many shapes and in many different degrees of precision. The building blocks of which they are composed — the constructs, the postulates, the assumptions — may be molar or molecular.[15]

Griffiths listed the following steps in theory development:

1. A *description* of administrative behaviors in one situation.
2. A *definition* of certain basic concepts.
3. A more *general statement* which is descriptive of average behavior in a limited number of situations.
4. A statement of one or more hypotheses.
5. An *evaluation* and *reconstruction* of the hypotheses inaccordance with later observations.
6. The statement of principles.[16]

[13]Andrew W. Halpin, *Theory and Research in Administration* (New York: The Macmillan Company, 1966).

[14]*Op. cit.*, p. 4.

[15]Andrew W. Halpin, "The Development of Theory in Educational Administration," *Administrative Theory in Education*, edited by Andrew W. Halpin (Chicago: Midwest Administration Center, University of Chicago, 1958), p. 5.

[16]Roald F. Campbell and Russell T. Gregg (eds.), *Administrative Behavior in Education* (New York: Harper and Row, 1957), pp. 363-364.

In a later writing, Griffiths presented the paradigm for theory development shown in Figure 3.

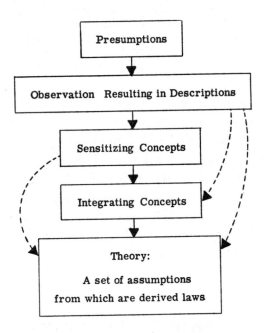

Figure 3. *Paradigm for theory development.* Adapted by permission from Daniel E. Griffiths," The Nature and Meaning of Theory," *Behavioral Science and Educational Administration,* Sixth-third Yearbook of the National Society for the Study of Education (Chicago: The University of Chicago Press, 1964), p. 104.

The foregoing illustrates the care and precision with which theorists in administration have been adhering to the kinds of rules for theorizing utilized in the behavioral sciences. The status of theory in administration is incomplete but promising. Much work has been done, but as one would expect, efforts on occasion have been at cross purposes with one another, oversimplified, or not sufficiently and carefully defined. Halpin described this condition well:

> In our efforts to develop theory in educational administration, we have been impeded by three substantive problems: (1) We have not been clear about the meaning of theory. (2) We have tended to be preoccupied with taxonomies and have confused these with theories. (3) We have not been sure of the precise domain of the theory we are seeking to devise.[17]

Despite these negative comments, Halpin demonstrated confidence that progress would continue to be made in theory development, and he included an elaborate paradigm for research on administrator behavior. Persumably, the research should lead to further theorizing efforts, and it will. There is no doubt that the individuals and groups who have toiled so arduously at theory building in educational administration have made a very real and substantive contribution toward the development of educational theory.

INSTRUCTIONAL THEORY

A more recent development in the area of sub-theories to educational theory is the rapid growth of thinking and research pertaining to instruction. Articles on pedagogy and reports of research on teaching have been with us for a long time, but few, until recently, claimed to lead toward theories of instruction.

Jerome S. Bruner's book, *The Process of Education,* touched off a great deal of dialogue about fundamental educational operations and conditions. The nature of instructional processes became a part of that dialogue. Then, in 1963, Bruner addressed the national conference of the

[17]*Theory and Research in Administration, op. cit.,* p. 6.

Association for Supervision and Curriculum Development on the subject of theory of instruction. An adaptation of this address was published in the official journal of the association. In that article Bruner proposed four aspects of a theory of instruction:

1. First, a theory of instruction should concern itself with the factors that predispose a child to learn effectively.
2. It should concern itself with optimal structuring of knowledge.
3. A third aspect of a theory of instruction deals with the optimal sequence that is required for learning.
4. Finally, a fourth aspect of a theory of instruction should concern itself with the nature and pacing of rewards and punishments and the successes and failures.[18]

Whether Bruner was causal or not, a flurry of activity under the general category of theories of instruction followed his presentation. Most of the activity was an inherent part of the ongoing program of the Association for Supervision and Curriculum Development. A sample of such activity merits attention here. Macdonald argued for a clarification of terms associated with instruction. As a beginning point, he suggested that a valid distinction be made among curriculum, instruction, and teaching. Having singled out instruction as an unique concept among the three terms, he then discussed as needs in research and theoretical work adequate models of instruction, empirical analysis and theory sifting from other areas, and the identification and description of criterion variables.[19]

Toward the end of 1963 and the beginning of 1964, the Association for Supervision and Curriculum Development sponsored its ninth Curriculum Research Institute. Papers

[18]Jerome S. Bruner, "A Theory of Instruction," *Educational Leadership*, 20: 523-532, May, 1963.

[19]James B. Macdonald, "The Nature of Instruction: Needed Theory and Research," *Educational Leadership*, 21:5-7, October, 1963.

from that institute were published in a pamphlet entitled *Theories of Instruction.*[20] It is not necessary for us to review all of the elements of this publication. Most of the papers were written from the particular research bias of the authors. Individual research programs were related to theory of instruction in all cases. A major point to note here is the emphasis on carefully controlled research as a basis for reaching generalizations about teaching, or instruction, whichever term is used. These papers are an excellent illustrations of the kinds of steps that need to be taken to build different theories in a given field, in this case, instruction.

A similar publication followed in 1966. This publication was an outgrowth of a joint seminar on teaching sponsored by the Association for Supervision and Curriculum Development and the Center for the Study of Instruction of the National Education Association. Here again, the emphasis was upon research in the classroom, and the authors of the included papers assumed diversified postures toward the character of research done.[21]

Also in 1966 Bruner published *Toward a Theory of Instruction.*[22] In it, Bruner expanded his previously announced or inferred theory of instruction. His point of departure was the major features of a theory of instruction which consisted of the same four included in an earlier article. The foregoing publications are very illustrative of initial efforts of individuals to define and to theorize about instruction.

The position paper of the Commission on Instructional Theory of the Association for Supervision and Curriculum Devel-

[20]James B. Macdonald and Robert R. Leeper (eds.), *Theories of Instruction* (Washington: Association for Supervision and Curriculum Development, NEA, 1965).

[21]*The Way Teaching Is* (Washington: Association for Supervision and Curriculum Development and the Center for the Study of Instruction, NEA, 1966).

[22]Jerome S. Bruner, *Toward a Theory of Instruction* (Cambridge: Harvard University Press, 1966).

opment might well provide a launching platform for even more intensified effort in the development of theories of instruction.[23] The position paper was a composite of the thoughts and ideas of the various Commission members. The Commission, conceiving instructional theory to be a very complex phenomenon, concluded that sub-theories should be built as supports for it. This position is very much in line with the one assumed in Chapter 2, namely, that complex theories are characterized by supporting sub-theories. After debating the pros and cons of philosophical and scientific theory, the Commission took the position that it would concern itself primarily with scientific theory. The Commission defined theory as follows:

> In this document the term theory is used in the sense in which it is used in the natural sciences to represent a set of interrelated generalizations, derived from data, which permit some degree of prediction or control over the phenomena to which they pertain. Thus a *theory of instruction* would be represented by a set of statements, based on sound replicable research, which would permit one to predict how particular changes in the educational environment would affect pupil learning.[24]

From this definition, it may be noted that research and the development of instructional theory need to be tied together. In this way theorists are encouraged to develop theories inductively from generalizations based on experimental data.

The position paper included a series of criteria which may apply to the analysis of any scientific theory, but in this case, they are focused upon the development of instructional

---

[23]Ira J. Gordon, Chairman, "Theories of Instruction: A Set of Guidelines (A position paper prepared by the Commission on Instructional Theory and presented at the Annual Conference of the Association for Supervision and Curriculum Development, NEA at Dallas, Texas in March, 1967).

[24]*Ibid.*, p. 5.

theory. The criteria are:

1. A statement of an instructional theory should include a set of postulates and definitions of terms involved in these postulates.
2. The statement of an instructional theory or sub-theory should make explicit the boundaries of its concern and the limitations under which it is proposed.
3. A theoretical construction must have internal consistency — a logical set of interrelationships.
4. An instructional theory should be congruent with empirical data.
5. An instructional theory must be capable of generating hypotheses.
6. An instructional theory must contain generalizations which go beyond the data.
7. An instructional theory must be verifiable.
8. An instructional theory must be stated in such a way that it is possible to collect data to disprove it.
9. An instructional theory must not only explain past events but also must be capable of predicting future events.
10. Propositions of the theory should be properly derived from the data on which they are based.[25]

From these observations about the emerging literature on instructional theory, it may be noted that individuals in leadership roles in the development of instructional theory are accepting the principle of scientific rigor as essential to theory building. In addition to the foregoing efforts, instructional theory has been greatly enhanced by extensive hard-nosed research. Standards for this research have been included in the *Handbook of Research on Teaching*.[26] There seems to be little question but that a great deal of leadership in the development of components of educational theory has been demonstrated by those working upon theory building in the area of instruction.

[25]*Ibid.*, pp. 16-23.

[26]N. L. Gage (ed.), *Handbook of Research on Teaching* (Chicago: Rand McNally and Company, 1963).

EDUCATIONAL THEORY

Since the publication of the first edition of this book, increased attention in educational theory has emerged. This new attention is focused upon the full meaning of education which is an important area of human knowledge. Whether it is termed a discipline or not is immaterial. The problem of educational theory, like that posed for any theory, is to explain its subject matter and the interrelationships among its constructs and generalizations. Education cannot be explained by prescriptive (philosophic) theory alone; descriptive (scientific) theory is required also.

An appeal for needed development in educational theory was well voiced by Broudy when he called for unifying principles to be used in the resolution of conflict associated with innovations in school practices. For Broudy, a unified theory of education would take into account the following factors:

> a. The present and projected kinds of knowledge and personality traits required for citizenship, vocation, and self development.
> b. A unified theory of education must be clear about the uses of schooling.
> c. A unified theory must be judicious about the latest developments in learning theory and teaching technology.
> d. A unified theory has to provide for general and special education, for differences in ability and bent.[27]

A much different approach to educational theory was taken by Brauner.[28] Brauner analyzed six major traditions that have influenced American educational thought throughout the Nation's history. The traditions and characteristics

[27]Harry S. Broudy, "Needed: A Unifying Theory of Education," *Curriculum Change: Direction and Process* (Washington: Association for Supervision and Curriculum Development, NEA, 1966), p. 24.

[28]Charles Brauner, *American Educational Theory* (Englewood Cliffs, N.J.: Prentice-Hall, Inc., 1964).

associated with them are presented in Figure 4. In the figure,

The Tradition	Method	View of Child	Controlling Theme
Monitorial Method	Drill and Memorization	Trainable beast	Obedience
Object-Teaching	Handling Things	Flower to be cultivated	Discovery
Herbartianism	Five Steps	Social Embryo to be molded	Will power
Child Study	Self-Expression	Potential Artist	Sensitivity
Experimentalism	Problem-Solving by Scientific Method	Responsible Rebel	Involvement
Current Academic Emphasis	New Technology	Greatest Natural Resource	Mastery

Figure 4. *Six major traditions in American Education.* Adapted by permission from Charles J. Brauner, *American Educational Theory* (Englewood Cliffs, N.J.: Prentice-Hall, Inc., 1964), p. 279.

it can be noted that method, view of the child, and a controlling theme are regarded by Brauner as the principal theoretical characteristics associated with the six traditions listed.

In addressing himself to the issue of education as a subject of analytical study, Brauner was critical of the present state of affairs. He said: "With but rare exceptions, the bulk of what is written about education fails in substance, form, and vocabulary. It fails as scholarship, as interpretation, as communication, and as guidance for instruction."[29] If Brauner's assessment is correct, educational theory rests on

[29]*Ibid.*, p. 302.

an unstable base. Yet educational theory is no less needed for that reason.

A growing theme in educational theorizing is the conception of education as a discipline. In the accompanying dialogue, the subject of education as a field of study, and/or as a field susceptible to theorizing, is germane. Two definitive works will be cited as examples.

A series of papers and responses to them was given at a symposium at John Hopkins University in May, 1961.[30] They were addressed to the question of whether education should be regarded as a discipline. Scholars representing various disciplines gave the papers and made comments upon the papers. Frequently, when an original paper posed education as a discipline, the comment took the opposite side. The arguments were conditioned by the ways individuals defined disciplines and related concepts. For example, a proponent of education as a discipline was opposed by a proponent of education as a profession. A discipline adds to its own knowledge; a profession is characterized by the services it renders. Education is the application of many disciplines; a discipline develops its own way of study and behaving. Obviously, the symposium was much more successful in identifying the issues involved than resolving them.

In the volume edited by Walton and Keuthe, a number of individuals with biases in their own fields of study debated and analyzed the disciplinary status of education. In yet another volume, a single author spelled out a detailed rationale for education as a discipline.[31] In the latter, Belth revived many of the arguments about why education should or should not be a discipline. He rejected the notion that education is solely the application of other disciplines, holding in-

[30]John Walton and James L. Kuethe (eds.), *The Discipline of Education* (Madison, Wis.: The University of Wisconsin Press, 1963).

[31]Marc Belth, *Education as a Discipline* (Boston: Allyn and Bacon, Inc., 1965).

stead that education is a field of study (a discipline) in its own right. Education as a set of "know how to do" technical skills was rejected in deference to education conceived as the development of powers of explanation. Belth stated:

> The study of education is the study of the way in which models for inquiry are constructed, used, altered, and reconstructed. It is, further, a study of the types of models available to us at any given moment, and the conditions which make the model either employable or in need of rebuilding.[32]

The following list of what the study of education would include helps visualize Belth's point of view:

1. A history of the theories and models of education. Their development and their careers.
2. Principles and procedures for analysis of educational models.
3. The exploration of the functions of the prevailing models for the tool skills of reading and writing.
4. The study of prevailing models, revealing the modes of thinking in social, psychological, economic, and political facets of our developed culture which have given that culture its characteristic patterns of operation. An intensive study of the relationship between ways of thinking and the developed culture patterns would set forth the determining force of thought and the characteristics of the elements which enter into the act of thinking.
5. Detailed study into the variety of models by means of which a particular subject discipline is undertaken or performed (a history and analysis of the models of a discipline, or of several disciplines). In this one area especially, the theoretically grounded teacher of social studies, for example, is able, if competent in analysis, to analyze the level of education which a child has reached.
6. A period which is like the widely prevailing student teaching practice, but which is a research program and an analytical seminar in which there is opportunity for diagnosis of the efforts of the prospective teacher, examining his own educational experiments in his classes.[33]

[32]*Ibid.*, p. 103.

[33]*Ibid.*, p. 304.

Although one may argue with the details of Belth's position, he nonetheless stimulates thought in regard to the disciplinary status of education.

It is not the purpose of this book to pursue the argument of whether education is a discipline or not. The belief that education is an organized field of study about which theories may be built, however, is another matter. There is an increasing demand for rigorous research and theory building in education. Pioneer steps in this direction were taken by individuals such as G. Stanley Hall and Edward L. Thorndike, who employed the techniques of science in solving educational problems. Most of what is done in schools, however, either is done on a trial-and-error basis or because practice has made it respectable. What is now needed is for clear-headed thinkers to stretch for more rational explanation of what education does and should do. Individuals who are convinced that the only worthwhile activities for students of professional education are intensive study of the organized disciplines and extensive practical experience in schools tend to lead education away from badly needed systematic study of itself. It really does not matter much whether education is called a discipline, a profession, or something else. Irrespective of label, evidence mounts that education is sufficiently mature to become an organized field of study.

A third kind of evidence for the advance of thinking about educational theory is reflected in the writing and research on the use of models in educational theorizing. The most extensive work over an extended period of time in this area was done by George and Elizabeth Maccia. The final report of their project brings together the essence of many previous reports.[34] Educational theory models were reproduced from

[34] Elizabeth Steiner Maccia and George S. Maccia, *Development of Educational Theory Derived from Three Educational Theory Models* (Columbus, Ohio: The Ohio State University Research Foundation 1966).

models from such areas as set theory, information theory, graph theory, and general systems theory. Ways of deducing educational research hypotheses were described by use of models and symbols borrowed from theoretical formulations external to education.

In educational theory as in administrative theory and instructional theory, we note again that attention is being increasingly paid to the rules for theory building as prescribed by behavioral scientists. These are real signs of mature development in an organized field of study. In terms of specific theory development, most products reflect descriptive (scientific) theorizing rather than prescriptive (philosophic or normative) theorizing. Both types of theorizing, however, are relevant for educational theory. The so-called "is-ought" dichotomy in educational thinking cannot be; it has to be "both." For schooling to be operative and meaningful, the factual and predictive questions about what may be done must be answered and these probably have to be answered first. Then the question of what shall we do or what ought we to do can be debated more intelligently.

SUMMARY

The purpose of this chapter was to describe theorizing activities in professional education. Five general headings representing discrete areas of activity were used as illustrations: theory and practice, theory and philosophy, theory in school administration, instructional theory, and educational theory.

Meaningful relationships may be established between the work of theorists and the work of practitioners, but theory and practice are not one and the same. Theory may direct practice, or it may explain the nature of practice. Conversely, data for theory may come from practice. Theories, in turn, are tested in the crucible of practice. The relationship is reciprocal.

Individuals frequently have used traits and names of philosophies of education and theories of education interchangeably. Dimensions of philosophy have much to contribute to educational theorizing both at the level of prescriptive and descriptive theory, but philosophy and theory are not coterminous domains.

An excellent example of educational theorizing at work is in the field of school administration. Administrative theory has been developed to its present stage as a sub-theory of educational theory. Theorists in adminstration have disciplined themselves to use basic rules for theorizing adopted from behavioral and social sciences.

Developments in the area of instructional theory are very encouraging. A substantial effort is being made to develop instructional theory as a sub-theory to educational theory. It is significant that the domain of theories of instruction is being discriminated from other potential areas of education such as administration and curriculum. It also is significant that theory development is being related to carefully designed research.

Finally, a demand for bringing together the theoretical work done in the sub-theories into total educational theory is increasing. Although the dimensions of educational theory are far from being clearly identified, the profession is attempting to develop more rational explanations for those it is able to identify. The impetus to sub-theory building, the use of models for directing thinking and explanation, and the thrust of theory-oriented research are evidences of healthy activity in the area of educational theory.

SUGGESTED READINGS

Administrative Theory. Austin, Texas: The University of Texas, 1961.

"A Symposium: Can the Laws of Learning Be Applied in the Classroom?" *Harvard Educational Review,* 29:83-117, Spring, 1959.

"A Symposium: What Can Philosophy Contribute to Educational Theory? *Harvard Educational Review,* 28:283-339, Fall, 1958.

Bayles, Ernest E. "Present Status of Educational Theory in the United States," *School and Society,* 87:5-8, January, 1059.

Bellack, Arno A., Herbert M. Kliebard, Ronald T. Hyman, and Frank L. Smith, Jr. *The Language of the Classroom.* New York: Teachers College Press, Teachers College, Columbia University, 1966.

Belth, Marc. *Education as A Discipline.* Boston: Allyn and Bacon, Inc., 1965.

Black, Hugh C. "A Four-fold Classification of Educational Theories," *Educational Theory,* 16:281-291, July, 1966.

Black, Hugh C. "Confusion and Conflict in Educational Theory: An Analysis, " *Peabody Journal of Education,* 30:153-160, November. 1952.

Brauner, Charles J. *American Educational Theory.* Englewood Cliffs, N.J.: Prentice-Hall, Inc., 1964.

Broudy, Harry S. "Needed: A Unifying Theory of Education," *Curriculum Change: Direction and Process,* Robert E. Leeper, editor. Washington: Association for Superivision and Curriculum Development, NEA, 1966, pp. 15-26.

Broudy, Harry S. and John R. Palmer. *Exemplars of Teaching Method.* Chicago: Rand McNally and Company, 1965.

Bruner, Jerome S. "Needed: A Theory of Instruction," *Educational Leadership,* 20:523-532, May, 1963.

Bruner, Jerome S. *The Process of Education.* Cambridge, Mass: Harvard University Press, 1960.

Bruner, Jerome S. *Toward A Theory of Instruction.* Cambridge, Mass.: Harvard University Press, 1966.

Burnett, Joe R. "Observations on the Logical Implications of Philosophic Theory for Educational Theory and Practice," *Educational Theory,* 11:65-70, April, 1961.

Clements, Millard. "Theory and Education," *Educational Theory.* 12:124-128, April, 1962.

Coladarci, Arthur P. and Jacob W. Getzels. *The Use of Theory in Educational Administration.* Stanford: School of Education, Stanford University, Monograph No. 5, 1955.

Downey, Lawrence W. "Organizational Theory as a Guide to Educational Change," *Educational Theory,* 11:38-44, January, 1961.

Fattu, Nicholas A. "Teacher Effectiveness," *NEA Journal,* 50:55-56, October, 1961.

Gage, N. L. (ed.). *Handbook of Research on Teaching.* Chicago: Rand McNally and Company, 1963.

Gowin, D. B. "Can Educational Theory Guide Practice?" *Educational Theory,* 13:6-12, January, 1963.

Gowin, D. B., G. L. Newsome, and K. A. Chandler. "A Scale to Study Logical Consistency of Ideas about Education," *Journal of Psychology,* 51:443-455, April, 1961.

Gordon, Ira J., Chairman. "Theories of Instruction: A Set of Guidelines." Mimeographed paper distributed by the Commission on Instructional Theory, Association for Supervision and Curriculum Development, Dallas, Texas, February, 1967.

Griffiths, Daniel E. *Administrative Theory.* New York: Appleton-Century-Crofts, Inc., 1959.

Griffiths, Daniel E. "The Nature and Meaning of Theory," *Behavioral Science and Educational Administration.* Sixth-third Yearbook of the National Society for the Study of Education. Chicago: The University of Chicago Press, pp. 95-118.

Halpin, Andrew W. (ed.). *Administrative Theory in Education.* Chicago: Midwest Administration Center, University of Chicago, 1958.

Halpin, Andrew W. *Theory and Research in Administration.* New York: The Macmillan Company, 1966.

Hughes, Marie M. "What Is Teaching? One Viewpoint," *Educational Leadership,* 19:251-258. January, 1962.

Maccia, Elizabeth Steiner and George S. Maccia. *Development of Educational Theory Derived from Three Educational Theory Models.* Columbus, Ohio: The Ohio State University Research Foundation, 1966.

Macdonald, James B. "The Nature of Instruction: Needed Theory and Research," *Educational Leadership,* 21:5-7, October, 1963.

Macdonald, James B. and Robert R. Leeper (eds.). *Theories of Instruction.* Washington: Association for Supervision and Curriculum Development, NEA, 1965.

Mason, Robert E. "Grounds of Acceptable Theory in Education," *Studies in Philosophy and Education*, 1:44-65.

Newsome, George L., Jr. "In What Sense Is Theory a Guide to Practice in Education?" *Educational Theory*, 14:31-39, January, 1964.

O'Connor, D. J. *An Introduction to the Philosophy of Education.* London: Routledge and Kegan Paul, 1957.

Page, Ellis B. "Behavioral Theory, Verbal Magic, and Education," *Educational Theory*, 12:73-83, April, 1962.

Perkinson, Henry J. "A Note on: 'Can Educational Theory Guide Practice?' " *Educational Theory*, 14:93-94, April, 1964.

School and Society, 87:1-20, January, 1959.

Skinner, B. F. "Why We Need Teaching Machines," *Harvard Educational Review.* 31:377-398, Fall, 1961.

Smith, B. Othanel and Robert H. Ennis (eds.). *Language and Concepts in Education.* Chicago: Rand McNally and Company, 1961.

Thelen, Herbert A. *Education and the Human Quest.* New York: Harper and Brothers, 1960.

Walton, John and James L. Kuethe (eds.). *The Discipline of Education.* Madison, Wis.: The University of Wisconsin Press, 1963.

The Way Teaching Is. Washington: Association for Supervision and Curriculum Development and the Center for the Study of Instruction, NEA, 1966.

4

DEVELOPMENTS IN

CURRICULUM THEORY

Progress in curriculum theory has been slow and meager. And like many other functions in education, the curriculum function has responded more to the external pressures from an expanding culture than to internal examination, systematic research, and explanation. In responding to the set of external forces, curriculum workers have been busy. They have worked diligently and at times, creatively. But too few curriculum workers have responded to the need for thoughtful theoretical work.

On a more positive side, there are some milestones that have been passed in an almost inevitable development of what properly may be called a field of curriculum theory. The major purpose of this chapter is to highlight selected of these developments. The details, arguments, and sub-items of curriculum theory will be discussed in later chapters.

MILESTONES IN CURRICULUM THEORY

One of the first references to be made to curriculum theory was in the 1927 yearbook of the National Society for the Study of Education.[1] The dimensions of curriculum theory were not outlined, but some authors claimed the various curriculum positions to be theories. There were many reasons for differences in position as exhibited by the Herbartian reaction to formal discipline and the disagreements between the Progressives and the Essentialists on the choice and organization of subject matters. In spite of the diverse opinions of the committee responsible for the yearbook, a general statement of working principles of curriculum-making was formulated. That statement of principles came as close to being a statement of curriculum theory as anything set forth up to that time.

The first large-scale discussion of curriculum theory took place at the University of Chicago in 1947. The papers presented at that conference were published in a monograph in 1950.[2] That publication stands as a signal work in curriculum theory and is one that should be read by all students of the field. Each author of a paper was given virtually complete freedom to treat his topic individually inasmuch as the composite of papers made no pretense at covering the field of curriculum theory comprehensively. It is significant to observe that in one of the overview sections of the report, the following three-fold task for curriculum theory was prescribed:

[1]Harold Rugg, Chairman, *The Foundations and Technique of Curriculum Construction,* Twenty-sixth Yearbook of the National Society for the Study of Education, Part I and II (Bloomington, Ill.: Public School Publishing Company, 1927).

[2]Virgil E. Herrick and Ralph W. Tyler (eds.), *Toward Improved Curriculum Theory,* Supplementary Educational Monograph, Number 71 (Chicago: University of Chicago Press, 1950).

(1) to identify the critical issues or points in curriculum development and their underlying generalizations; (2) to point up the relationships which exist between these critical points and their supporting structure; and (3) to suggest and to forecast the future of approaches made to resolve these critical issues.[3]

And in a concluding chapter the following challenge was issued:

As a further effort in hastening the communications between groups of interested people and in the development of more adequate theory, someone might spend time trying to describe the nature of such theory, its tasks, its subject matter, its tests, and its uses.[4]

At least in partial-response to that challenge, the first edtion of this book (*Curriculum Theory*) appeared in 1961. It was the first single volume to present an organized statement of the status and dimensions of curriculum theory based upon conceptual structures and relationships derived from theory building efforts in closely related disciplines. It is not necessary for us to review the particular concepts or arguments presented in it because most of them also are contained in this volume. But the occurrence of the publication is of historical significance here.

A number of papers and articles have appeared since 1961 that have contributed significantly to increased understanding of the dimensions and problems of curriculum theorizing. Two of these were given at the 1963 National Conference of the Association for Supervision and Curriculum Development. The conference, in part, consisted of a series of seminars one of which had curriculum theory as its topic. Two papers were given at the seminar which pointed up a major dilema in curriculum theory, and the dilema remains unresolved at this writing. The paper titles reveal the two sides. One of the papers was given by Beauchamp wherein he

[3]*Ibid.*, p. 1.

[4]*Ibid.*, p. 121.

analyzed the approach of the scientist to the tasks of theory building in curriculum.[5] In this presentation, curriculum theory was related conceptually to theory building in other domains of knowledge. The basic principles common to all, as seen by the scientist, were stressed. Careful and consistent use of technical terminology, analysis and classification of knowledge and conjecture, and the use of predictive research to increase the number of firm generalizations, or laws, were cited as principles that would give better explanation for curriculum phenomena.

The second paper has as its theme the role of philosophy in the development of scientific curriculum theory.[6] In the paper, Smith outlined three principal tasks with which philosophy can deal in aiding the curriculum theorist: (1) to formulate and justify educational purposes, (2) to select and organize knowledge, and (3) to deal with verbal traps. In identifying these three tasks, Smith noted several weaknesses in the development of curriculum theory. Too frequently, he said, curriculum theorists fail to recognize the interrelationships between educational objectives and the content of a school program. Sometimes the content itself becomes an objective, or a series of objectives. Too often, criteria for selection of content or objectives are not apparent, if they exist at all. In selecting content, a curriculum theorist must take into account the nature and structure of knowledge. He will be at great disadvantage if he fails to discriminate among factual information, values, and general principles. All of these kinds of problems are intimately related to the language used in curriculum theorizing. Progress is inhibited

---

[5]George A. Beauchamp, "Developing a Scientific Theory in Curriculum." A paper presented at the national conference of the Association for Supervision and Curriculum Development, NEA, St. Louis, Missouri, 1963.

[6]B. Othanel Smith, "The Role of Philosophy in the Development of Scientific Curriculum Theory." A paper presented at the national Conference of the Association for Supervision and Curriculum Development, NEA, St. Louis, Missouri, 1963.

when basic concepts that are repeatedly used need clarification.

We note here that these two papers brought several facets of curriculum theory into sharp focus. One is that theorizing about curriculum is not solely a matter of establishing facts and relationships among empirical data. More than that, the theorist must be concerned with choices and the consequences of those choices, and at this point, the world of values confronts him. The theorist is concerned with choices at the levels of selection of purposes and content in response to those purposes. Science is of little help to him here. However, a disciplined language is a necessity whether he is calling upon the techniques of science or the wisdom of philosophy.

The use of models in theoretical work also has invaded curriculum theory efforts. A very useful contribution in this area was made by Macdonald in a paper given at a meeting of professors of curriculum.[7] In this paper, Macdonald distinguished four systems prevalent in schooling: curriculum, instruction, teaching, and learning. By use of a Venn-type diagram, he identified the interactions of the four systems. Then he analyzed the curriculum system using a general systems model characterized by the components of input, content and process, output, and feedback. At least two unique ideas emerge from Macdonald's paper. One is that we can clarify our thinking about curriculum if it is identified as an unique system of schooling. The other is that the use of the general system approach helps to define the kind and scope of conceptualizations needed in curriculum theory.

A slightly different schema for schooling was developed by Broudy, Smith, and Burnett. It is shown in Figure 5. In it,

[7]James B. Macdonald, "Curriculum Theory: Problems and A Prospectus," Mimeographed, a paper presented at the Professors of Curriculum meeting, Miami Beach, April, 1964.

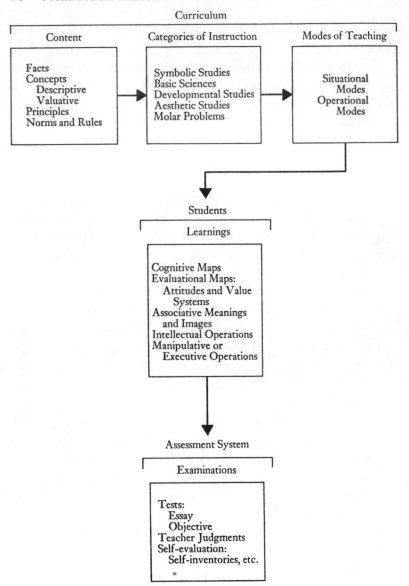

Figure 5. *A schema for schooling.* Adapted by permission from Harry S. Broudy, B. Othanel Smith, and Joe R. Burnett, *Democracy and Excellence in American Secondary Education* (Chicago: Rand McNally and Company, 1964), p. 78.

curriculum is depicted as part of a total system of influence directed at students. Modes of teaching are included as part of the curriculum components in the diagram, but in the text in which it appears, the authors stated: "Although modes of teaching are not, strictly speaking, a part of the curriculum, for practical purposes it is not useful to ignore them entirely in curriculum theory."[8] This statement would lead us to believe that Broudy, Smith, and Burnett would not significantly disagree with Macdonald's distinction between curriculum and teaching.

Beauchamp reviewed the progress made in curriculum theory between the years 1960 and 1965.[9] As a framework for discussing the research and writings about curriculum theory, he identified six components of curriculum as a field of study. These were foundational influences, subject matters, curriculum design, curriculum engineering, evaluation and research, and theory building. He noted that most progress was being made in the areas of subject matters and curriculum engineering.

Faix applied structural-functional analysis as derived from biology, sociology and anthropology to the task of refining curriculum concepts. A curriculum function was described as what is done; a curriculum structure, as how it is done. In other words, curriculum functions describe the process by which curriculum structures are maintained or changed. A list of questions raised by a structural-functional analysis of curriculum phenomena was presented, and the titles and sub-titles of the list were termed a tentative classification of curriculum phenomena. They were: (1) general questions about curriculum phenomena, (2) questions about a curric-

[8]*Ibid.*, p. 79.

[9]George A. Beauchamp, "Progress in Curriculum Theory 1960-1965." Mimeographed: a paper presented at the annual conference of the American Educational Research Association, NEA, Chicago, 1965.

ulum system, (3) questions about units of analysis and elements, (4) questions about the structure of a curriculum system, (5) questions about the functions of a curriculum system, (6) questions about curriculum processes, and (7) general questions about structural-functional analysis procedures.[10] Since classification is a foundational step in scientific theory construction, this contribution warrants attention and development.

Maccia analyzed four types of curriculum theory: curriculum theory (event theory), formal curriculum theory, valuational curriculum theory, and praxiological curriculum theory.[11] Curriculum theory (event theory) was described as the sorting out and characterizing events and relating them. In this connection, Maccia suggested that curriculum could be subsumed by a theory of instruction, thereby intimating that curriculum theory should be a sub-theory of instructional theory. Formal curriculum theory is focused on the structure of curriculum content. Valuational curriculum theory is concerned with the issue of what instructional content is the most valuable to present. And praxiological curriculum theory is speculation about appropriate curriculum means for reaching curriculum objectives. We may not agree with Maccia that so many labels are needed, or with the meanings she has assigned to curriculum, but she does help us to see more clearly that curriculum theory has several dimensions such as classification, design, values, and operations all of which must be accounted for in a full explanation of curriculum theory.

[10]Thomas L. Faix, "Structural-Functional Analysis as a Conceptual System for Curriculum Theory and Research: A Theoretical Study, "Mimeographed: a paper presented at the annual meeting of the American Educational Research Association, NEA, Chicago, 1966.

[11]Elizabeth Steiner Maccia, "Curriculum Theory and Policy." Mimeographed: a paper presented at the annual meeting of the American Educational Research Association, NEA, Chicago, 1965.

A very interesting analysis of the use of definitions and models in curriculum theorizing was made by Johnson.[12] Whereas Maccia had implied that the definition of curriculum should emerge from the results of theory building, Johnson insisted upon a definition of curriculum as a directive force for the theory builder. He claimed that past efforts in curriculum theory have been either programmatic or analytical and that the programmatic works have been concerned with curriculum positions with primary emphasis upon curriculum development. Johnson distinguished between curriculum and the process of curriculum development. For him, a curriculum is the output of a curriculum development system, but the curriculum development system is not curriculum. We clarify this a little more by noting that Johnson depicted curriculum as a structured series of intended learning outcomes. Curriculum so conceived relates to what pupils should learn rather than what they do. Under this definition, experiences that pupils have under the jurisdiction of a school become part of the domain of instruction. Like Faix, Johnson winds up his analysis with a six-point schema for curriculum:

1. A curriculum is a structured series of intended learning outcomes.
2. *Selection* is an essential aspect of curriculum formulation.
3. *Structure* is an essential characteristic of curriculum.
4. Curriculum guides instruction.
5. Curriculum evaluation involves validation of both selection and structure.
6. Curriculum is the criterion for instructional evaluation.[13]

Others before Johnson have depicted a curriculum as the output of a curriculum system and the input of an instructional system. It is necessary for a system to have both input

[12]Mauritz Johnson, Jr., "Definitions and Models in Curriculum Theory," *Educational Theory*, 17: 127-140, April, 1967.

[13]*Ibid.*, pp. 136-139.

and output geared to the feedback from evaluation in order to maintain the steady state that is characteristic of a system. It is most unusual that the curriculum system should be excluded from curriculum theory, however. It would appear that Johnson is making an appeal for definition of curriculum that will settle some of the arguments about curriculum design. No one would argue with him about the right to delineate design characteristics, but a good case can be made that design is only one facet of a total field called curriculum theory. Curriculum development is as much a part of curriculum theory as is curriculum design or any other subordinate question associated with the field of curriculum. Nevertheless, we are indebted to Johnson for helping to sharpen up the relationship between a curriculum and a curriculum development system, on the one hand, and for the admonishment on the other hand, that our notions about curriculum design do influence discrimination between sub-systems of schooling, particularly curriculum and evaluation.

Frymier reported on a series of discussions about curriculum theory held with his colleagues at Ohio State University.[14] He took the position that curriculum consists of three basic elements: actors, artifacts, and operations. Actors, according to Frymier, are persons directly involved with curriculum. Artifacts are the content of the curriculum including design problems. Operations are the processes involving the the interaction of actors and artifacts. The basic unit for study in curriculum is to include three phases: (1) that which is planned, (2) that which occurs, and (3) the evaluation. It can be noted from these three phases of the basic unit for curriculum study that Frymier and his colleagues interpret curriculum much more broadly than would Macdonald,

[14]Jack R. Frymier, "Around and Around the Curriculum Bush or In Quest of Curriculum Theory." A paper presented at the meeting of Professors of Curriculum, Dallas, Texas, 1967.

Johnson, or the present writer. According to this position both curriculum and instruction are subsumed by curriculum theory. The position raises certain questions. For example, does curriculum embrace all of the sub-systems of schooling? If instruction is to be accounted for within curriculum theory, why exert effort to define the dimensions of instructional theory? A major difficulty in theorizing within education is the dismal lack of well-developed educational theories that identify the sub-theory structure of education. The contrast between the positions taken by Johnson and Frymier, as two examples, serves as testimonial.

By no stretch of the imagination do the foregoing examples of work in curriculum theory represent all of the theorizing efforts in the general domain of curriculum. They are, however, illustrations of attempts to describe a field of endeavor that may be called curriculum theory. Thus far, no mention has been made of writings principally concerned with a single, or subordinate aspect, of curriculum theory such as curriculum design or curriculum planning. These will be treated later in individual chapters. At this point, however, it should be fruitful to structure the characteristics of curriculum theory.

CURRICULUM THEORY AND ITS INGREDIENTS

From the generalizations made in Chapter 2, two kinds of guide or principle emerge to help interested observers determine whether or not any given educational element is a curriculum element. One of these has to do with definition and theory content; the other, with the kinds of activity permissible or mandatory for individuals interested in theory building.

Definitions and Theory Content

Initially, we stated that a theory is a set of statements. It must be in the form of a physical record that may be used as a means of communication among people and as a directive force in furthering theoretical and practical work efforts. Individual statements within a theory must be related in such a way as to produce greater meaning to the individual parts and to foster interrelation among the parts, thereby extending meaning to the whole set of events giving rise to the theory. This demand for relatedness is present in all serious writing about theory. Most series of events in curriculum are so variable that explanations for them may need to assume the form of definition, hypothesis, postulate, assumption, fact, or theorem. In order for a theory to explain systematically these variant events, the theory builder needs to relate them.

Theory may be defined as a set of related statements that are arranged in such a manner as to give functional meaning to a series of events. The set of related statements may take the form of descriptive or functional definitions, operational constructs, assumptions, postulates, hypotheses, generalizations, laws, or theorems. The precise contents are dictated by the scope of the series of events, the amount of empirical knowledge available, and the degree of sophistication of theory and research surrounding the series of events.

Now to apply these basic ideas about theoretical work to curriculum theory. The first task is to define curriculum theory. If a theory is a set of related statements that are arranged so as to give functional meaning to a set or a series of events, *a curriculum theory is a set of related statements that gives meaning to a school's curriculum by pointing up the relationships among its elements and by directing its development, its use, and its evaluation.* A series of events for curriculum theory may be the meanings associated with a curriculum, with the use of a curriculum, with the development of a curriculum, with a curriculum design, with curriculum evaluation, and so forth.

Such series of events are only part of the task of identifying curriculum theory ingredients. Within each of any identified series of events, there are technical terms that define the subject matter of the theoretical field. These have to be defined, or the boundaries of the theorist's work cannot be determined. Definitions also serve an operational purpose when they can be translated into operational constructs in research.

When a theorist identifies pertinent technical concepts, he is forced to open up all aspects of the field of curriculum that need to be explained by a full-blown curriculum theory. When the theorist turns to definition of concepts, it immediately becomes apparent to him that the key concept demanding clear definition is curriculum. To anyone who has read a great deal of curriculum literature, it should be apparent that the word "curriculum" is used in three key ways. One use of the word "curriculum" is as a substantive phenomenon. In the frame of this usage, one talks about *a curriculum*, In most cases a curriculum is a plan of some kind. It may be a plan consisting of learning experiences for school pupils. If one accepts the definition quoted earlier from Mauritz Johnson, a curriculum is a set of intended outcomes. For others, a curriculum may be an elaborate document including objectives, activities, instructional materials, and time schedules. Some conceive a curriculum as a written document; others view it as a set of verbal agreements. One authority may propose that a curriculum be made for a school or a school district. Another may propose that one be made for a state's schools. A third may propose that a curriculum should be national in scope. Regardless of meanings associated, it is common to talk about *a curriculum.*

A second use of the word "curriculum" is as a synonym for *a curriculum system.* A curriculum system is the organized framework within a school or a school system within which all curriculum decisions are made. A curriculum system consists of the personnel organization and the organized procedures needed to produce a curriculum, to implement it, to appraise it, and to modify it in light of experience. The principal output of a curriculum system is a curriculum; the function of the system is to keep the curriculum dynamic.

A third use of the word "curriculum" is as a synonym for an area of professional study. This mode is to speak of *curriculum as a total field of study.* This is the usage employed by nearly all professional schools of education.

A very important and substantive part of the content of any theory is the accumulation of statements describing relationships among the ingredients of the theory. To these need to be added the structural relationships between the theory being developed and its sub-theories.

If we employ the three uses of curriculum as a framework, relationships among the ingredients of curriculum theory may be more readily identified. Within the concept of a curriculum, there are many key relationships to be described. The primary ones have to do with such matters as the relationships between goals and subject matters, between school organization and scope and sequence, or between subjects and overall design. Secondary, or peripheral, relationships have to do with influences that impinge on curriculum decisions but which are not a part of a curriculum. Statements of these relationships need to explain why primary decisions are made. For example, goals are selected according to a conceived role of the school in society. Much of grade placement of subject matter depends upon predictions about the school population.

The concept of a curriculum system implies a governing cluster of relationships. Most of them have to do with the human engineering required in the process of curriculum development and curriculum usage. The fundamental tasks of a curriculum system set the framework for needed relationship ties. Briefly (these will be discussed in detail in later chapters) the tasks inherent in a curriculum system are: (1) the choice of arena for curriculum decision-making, (2) the selection and involvement of persons in curriculum planning, (3) organization for and techniques used in curriculum planning, (4) actual writing of a curriculum, (5) implementing the curriculum, (6) evaluating the curriculum, and (7) providing for feedback and modification of the curriculum. When statements of relationship among these elements are articulated, the phenomena of curriculum development, curriculum use, and curriculum evaluation will have been described. The primary concern here is one of explaining the structure and functions of a curriculum system.

The purpose of curriculum as a field of study is to advance knowledge about curriculums and curriculum systems. Whatever is included in the field of study must be defended on the basis of that purpose. It is conventional for students of curriculum to study social and psychological foundations of education. Advanced students study research design and procedures in depth. They study and analyze out past experiences in curriculum affairs. Relationship ties among such studies and the basic ideas of a curriculum and a curriculum system give great theoretical strength to curriculum as a field of study.

To the foregoing relationship statements, others need to be added to fill out the picture of theory content in curriculum. These constitute the statements needed to show relationships between curriculum theory and the remaining sub-theories of educational theory. Figure 1 in Chapter 1 reveals some of these to be instructional theory, evaluation theory, administrative theory, and counseling theory. Relationship ties among some of these are stronger than among others. Irrespective of strength, relationships need to be described in order to clarify the unique role of curriculum theory as a sub-theory of educational theory.

These relationship statements have several forms depending on their nature. As stated earlier, the statements may appear as definitions, hypotheses, laws, or theorems. The quest for new and better relationships is the domain of research in curriculum theory.

Curriculum Theory-Building Activities

The curriculum theorist is subject to the same rules of behavior as any theorist in the behavioral sciences; consequently, he is obligated to engage in the most commonly accepted work practices of all. They are: (1) establishment of descriptive and prescriptive definitions for technical terms, (2) classification of existing and new knowledge, (3) inferential and predictive research, (4) sub-theory development, and development and use of models.

We have labored over the need for establishing and using definitions of technical terms to this point sufficiently to obviate the need for further development here. Generally, educational writers and theorists have been unwilling or unable to define their technical terms with care and to use them consistently once having defined them. It is absolutely essential for the theorist to identify and define the key terms of his field. For instance, such concepts as curriculum, subject matter, design, implementation, and evaluation are a few that would have to be carefully structured. These concepts permeate curriculum considerations. Furthermore, their careful and consistent use may well constitute the missing link in the conceptual chain of theoretical deliberations. Some of the works cited earlier in this chapter give evidence of a recognized need for this activity and of an increasing willingness on the part of some to engage in it. This is a most encouraging trend.

The act of classifying knowledge is another theory function. Although a classification system is not synonymous with a theory, the one is essential to the other. Without order and relationship, meaning for a series of events is elusive or non-existent.

Although some classification of curriculum knowledge has taken place in subordinate aspects of curriculum, a systematic classification is still lacking. This condition is strange because classification is a theory building activity that is very possible in the field of curriculum. Limited attempts have been made by those who have raised questions that curriculum theory should answer, such as those about what content, what organization, what teaching, for what pupils, for what purposes. Progress beyond that has been inhibited by the lack of acceptance of a conceptual framework for curriculum classification. The present writer is convinced that lack of advance in classification is primarily attributable to great variation in use of technical terms. The effect is to produce a reluctance to postulate a classification scheme and expose it to the light of research and experience.

Inference and prediction are of the highest order in the work of the theorizer. It is possible for one to arrive at definitions, descriptions, and classification schemes initially by analytical procedures or by simple descriptive research, but it is not possible for one to go beyond those levels without the kinds of research that will allow one to infer or predict from the results. The kinds of research from which inference and prediction may be made are assigned various names in research literature. We will note here only the two most relevant research techniques. First, it should be stated that the act of inferring is a logical process. An inference is a proposition or generalization derived from evidence by reasoning. The research design does not provide the inference.

With one type of problem, a researcher is concerned with the examination of differences between, or among, samples taken from a known population. Measures for a criterion, or dependent, variable are taken from all samples, and various treatments are assigned to individual sample groups so as to manipulate independent variable effects. The researcher, in these cases usually seeks causal relationships between the criterion variable and the independent variables. It is common for analysis of variance designs and techniques to be used in these cases to examine the relationships. The researcher reaches a conclusion from observation of the results of his data treatment. Providing he is satisfied with the validity and reliability of his conclusion, the researcher can infer that his conclusion is generalizable to all samples of the population. A simple illustration in curriculum research would be a study of the effects of various kinds of inservice training administered to randomly selected groups of teachers upon their ability to participate as curriculum planners. The results, assuming proper controls and treatments, would permit the researcher to infer that the same status would hold for other similarly chosen groups and their parent population.

In a sense prediction is a special case of inference. For predictive relationships, research is designed so that one can estimate the unknown from the known. However, it is first necessary to establish the relationship between the known and the unknown characteristics or behaviors. A commonly-used research technique for this kind of problem is correlational analysis. A study is made of the correlation between two or more sets of behaviors or characteristics that are assumed to be related. The purpose of such a study is to establish the strength of the relationship so that thereafter one can predict one of the sets of behaviors or characteristics (the unknown) from the other (the known). The well-known correlation between measures of intelligence and measures of school achievement was observed, and we feel confident, within established limits, that we can predict school achievement once intelligence has been measured satisfactorily. In curriculum, many needs for research of this kind exist. A curriculum itself is an expression of prediction. Curriculum planners predict that teachers will use a curriculum as a point of departure for their teaching; otherwise there would be little point in doing all that work. Curriculum planners may predict that certain learning outcomes will occur. Rarely have these things been tested out in research, but they must be to develop generalizations about the phenomena for purposes of building curriculum theory.

A mature theory is undergirded by sub-theories. If they seek mature curriculum theories, curriculum theorists must work at identifying and building the sub-theories of curriculum. What the sub-theories may be are dependent upon the concepts and procedures the theorist wishes to associate with the field of curriculum. Curriculum design is one possibility for a sub-theory to curriculum theory. Procedures for curriculum planning and implementation is another. Curriculum evaluation is a third. Accounting for these functions theoretically is the domain of sub-theory building in curriculum.

Model building is another activity for the curriculum theorist. Since models may be used to describe or explain simple and complex phenomena, they may be used at any level in curriculum. Models may be constructed to describe what a curriculum will look like or how it is to be used. Models may be developed to illustrate the components and interrelationships of a curriculum system within schooling. They may be constructed so as to direct the development of curriculum theory. It makes little difference whether models are "borrowed" from other areas of knowledge or whether they are developed indigenously within the framework of curriculum constructs.

SUMMARY

The central thesis of this chapter has been that description, explanation, and prediction are as applicable and necessary to curriculum theory as to any other field of endeavor. Most curriculum theorists will agree. They will also agree that the most basic theory-building activities are definition of technical terms, classification of knowledge, inference and prediction from research data, sub-theory building, and model making.

The heat of debate in curriculum theory is not so much upon theory building functions as it is upon to what the functions are to be applied. There is still much disagreement as to meanings to be associated with the word "curriculum," and to a substantial degree, the areas of disagreement inhibit theory building. Definitions about curriculum have cluttered the literature for decades, but they have failed dismally as catalysts for research leading to description, explanation, or prediction. It may be helpful to think in terms of the more obvious ways in which the word "curriculum" is used, namely, as *a curriculum, a curriculum system, and curriculum as a field of study.* The focal point of all curriculum endeavor is the development and use of a curriculum. Somehow a curriculum has to be developed and used. Some system for doing these things needs to be created. Knowledge about how to develop, to use, and to evaluate a curriculum defines curriculum as a field of study.

In this chapter, we have avoided lengthy discussion of the theoretical issues of curriculum design, the human engineering essential to a curriculum system, and the characteristics of curriculum as a field of study. The extended discussion has been reserved for the following three chapters for it is from these areas that the sub-theories of curriculum theory ultimately will be developed.

SUGGESTED READINGS

American Educational Research Association. "Curriculum Planning and Development," *Review of Educational Research*, 33:227-337, June, 1963.

American Educational Research Association. "Curriculum Planning and Development," *Review of Educational Research*, 36:339-398. June, 1966.

Anderson, Dan W., James B. Macdonald, and Frank B. May (eds.). *Strategies of Curriculum Development.* Columbus, Ohio: Charles E. Merrill Books, 1965.

Beauchamp, George A. *The Curriculum of the Elementary School.* Boston: Allyn and Bacon, Inc., 1964.

Beauchamp, George A. "Curriculum Theory Applied to Urban Schools," *Education in Urban Society*, B. J. Chandler, Lindley J. Stiles, and John I. Kitsuse, editors. New York: Dodd, Mead and Company, 1962, pp. 179-192.

Broudy, Harry S., B. Othanel Smith, and Joe R. Brunett. *Democracy and Excellence in American Secondary Education.* Chicago: Rand McNally and Company, 1964.

Dungan, James R. and Reginald T. Hinely. "What Does a Course in Curriculum Theory Accomplish?" *Journal of Educational Research*, 57:80-83, October, 1963.

Eisner, Elliot W. "Franklin Bobbitt and the 'Science' of Curriculum Making," *The School Review*, 75:29-47, Spring, 1967.

Elliott, David Loucks. *Curriculum Development and History as a Discipline.* Doctor's thesis. New York: Columbia University, 1963.

Faix, Thomas Llewellyn. *Toward a Science of Curriculum: Structural-functional Analysis as a Conceptual System for Theory and Research.* Doctor's thesis. Madison: University of Wisconsin, 1964.

Fisher, Carol Mae. *A Personal Approach to Curriculum Theory.* Doctor's thesis. Columbus: Ohio State University, 1966.

Ford, G. W. and Lawrence Pugno (eds.). *The Structure of Knowledge and the Curriculum.* Chicago: Rand McNally and Company, 1964.

Goodlad, John I. "The Organizing Center in Curriculum Theory and Practice," *Theory into Practice,* 1:215-221, October, 1962.

Herrick, Theral T. "Curriculum Problems: Some Basic Issues," *Teachers College Record,* 60:242-244, February, 1950.

Johnson, Mauritz, Jr. "Definitions and Models in Curriculum Theory," *Educational Theory,* 17:127-140. April, 1967.

Macdonald, James B. *Some Contributions of a General Behavior Theory for Curriculum.* Doctor's thesis. Madison: University of Wisconsin, 1956.

Parsons, Howard L. "The Humanities and the Curriculum," *Educational Theory,* 11:26-37, January, 1961.

Rugg, Harold, Chairman. *The Foundations and Technique of Curriculum-Construction.* Twenty-sixth Yearbook of the National Society for the Study of Education, Parts I and II. Bloomington, Ill.: Public School Publishing Company, 1927.

Smith, B. Othanel, William O. Stanley, and J. Harlan Shores. *Fundamentals of Curriculum Development.* Revised edition. Yonkers-on-Hudson: World Book Company, 1957.

5

CURRICULUM DESIGN

In the last chapter, it was established that the word "curriculum" is used in three ways: (1) as a curriculum, (2) as a system of schooling, and (3) as a field of study. The focal point of all curriculum effort is upon the first of these — a curriculum conceived as a substantive document. The purpose for having a curriculum system is to produce a curriculum and make it work. Curriculum as a field of study is designed to improve and advance knowledge about curriculums and their development and use. It is therefore logical that a discussion of specific theoretical problems begin with those associated with curriculums.

The theoretical issues associated with the concept of curriculum as a document (as a curriculum, that is) fall under the heading of *curriculum design*. It is the design characteristic that makes one curriculum like or different from another. There are two fundamental dimensions of curriculum design. The first has to do with the total content and arrangement of the document. The second is in reality a part of the first; it is the organized expression of the subject matters. Both of these dimensions circumscribe subordinate parts. We should keep in mind that the technical terms and statements used to describe a curriculum constitute the theoretical language of curriculum design. The focus of language to explain curriculum design is upon the two dimensions. Each of these merits full discussion because they are so critical to curriculum theory and research.

THE CONTENTS OF A CURRICULUM

Literature on curriculum is replete with discussions about definitions of curriculum, curriculum decision-making, curriculum planning, curriculum strategy, and so forth, but very little of it describes the finished product of such endeavor. In other words, organized descriptions of curriculum *designs* are not plentiful. For many years the writer has insisted that a curriculum is a written document. This point of view, when countered, is usually challanged by statements to the effect that the curriculum is not a written document or that it is "more than" a written document. What the curriculum is, if it is not a written document, or exactly what in it rises above a written document, those taking a stand do not make clear.

Content by Definition

Virtually all writers on the subject of curriculum have been compelled to define curriculum. There is much variance in the ways curriculum is defined even though subsequent discussions may be quite similar. This variance reveals itself in the following samples of selected definitions. Buswell used the term to mean "whatever content is used purposely by the school as a stimulus to learning."[1] Smith, Stanley and Shores stated:

> A sequence of potential experiences is set up in the school for the purpose of disciplining children and youth in group ways of thinking and acting. This set of experiences is referred to as the *curriculum*.[2]

A similar definition was offered by Beauchamp in his portrayal of curriculum as the design of a social group for the educational experiences of their children in school.[3] Krug stated that a curriculum "consists of the means of instruction used by the school to provide opportunities for student learning experiences leading to desired learning outcomes."[4] Ragan used the term curriculum "to include all of the experiences for which the school accepts responsibility."[5] Faunce and Bossing gave a similar definition.[6] Wagner stated that "Whatever it is that a child learns under the guidance and direction of the school is 'his' curriculum."[7] Others have held a similar point of view. Hopkins indicated that each child makes his own curriculum from the school environment.[8] Miel

[1]G. T. Buswell, "Organization and Sequence of the Curriculum," *The Psychology of Learning*, National Society for the Study of Education, Forty-first Yearbook, Part II (Bloomington, Ill.: Public School Publishing Company, 1942), p. 446.

[2]B. Othanel Smith, William O. Stanley, and J. Harlan Shores, *Fundamentals of Curriculum Development* (revised edition; Harcourt, Brace, and World, Inc., 1957), p. 3.

[3]George A. Beauchamp, *The Curriculum of the Elementary School* (Allyn Bacon, Inc., 1964), p. 15.

[4]Edward A. Krug, *Curriculum Planning* (revised edition; New York: Harper and Brothers, 1957), p. 3.

[5]William B. Ragan, *Modern Elementary Curriculum* (third edition; New York: Holt, Rinehart and Winston, Inc., 1966), p. 4.

[6]Roland C. Faunce and Nelson L. Bossing, *Developing the Core Curriculum* (second edition; Englewood Cliffs: Prentice-Hall, Inc., p. 115.

[7]Guy Wagner, "A Present Day Look at the American School Curriculum," *Education*, 78:328, February, 1958.

[8]L. T. Hopkins, "Who Makes the Curriculum?" *Teachers College Record*, 52:277, February, 1951.

made a distinction between the curriculum of each child and the old curriculum or the course of study? It is interesting to note here that Foshay attributed the many interpretations of curriculum after 1930 to a single basic idea, which was the concept of experience promulgated by John Dewey.[10] Such variation in definition led Beauchamp to conclude that there have been represented in the literature three discrete sets of associations with the concept, curriculum; namely, the experience notion, the social design notion, and the psychological notion.[11] Even though the discreteness of these differences has not been elaborated, one must conclude that the existence of difference in definition should set the stage for differences in curriculum design and in curriculum theory.

All of this argument about meanings associated with curriculum is centered in two basic ideas. We have already presented one in depicting curriculum differentially as a curriculum, a curriculum system, and a field of study. The number and complexity of the referents here are contributory to confusion in communication. The second, and probably the real fly in the ointment, is the word "experiences." Most attempts in recent decades at defining curriculum focus on the concept of experience. The key phrase in almost all definitions of curriculum is "experience" or "learning experience," and in most cases the definition of curriculum, under close scrutiny, reduces itself to a redefinition of learning. Learning is something a pupil does. Only the learner can have a learning experience. The task of the curriculum planner is to es-

[9] Alice M. Miel, "The School Curriculum in a Changing Culture," *Education Digest*, 21:21. November, 1955.

[10] Arthur W. Foshay, "Changing Interpretations of the Elementary Curriculum," *The American Elementary School*, Thirteenth Yearbook of the John Dewey Society, edited by Harold G. Shane (New York: Harper and Brothers, 1953), p. 17.

[11] George A. Beauchamp, "Curriculum Organization and Development in Historical Perspective," *Review of Educational Research*, 27:245, June, 1957 .

tablish an environment in which the learner *may have* a learning experience. The curriculum planner can only anticipate the conditions under which learners may have learning experiences. Another use of experience seems to be as a substitute for the word "activity," but when this is the case the curriculum planner may, if he wishes, consider the setting forth of an array of activities as part of the curriculum being designed.

Design and Schooling

Conceivably it will be helpful for us to look at some of the dynamics of the schooling situation for cues for curriculum design features. Important social institutions like schools may be justified only in terms of the goals or purposes they are intended to serve. Once goals are recognized and accepted, means must be selected for the attainment of the goals. Let us use Figure 6 as a model for illustrating these

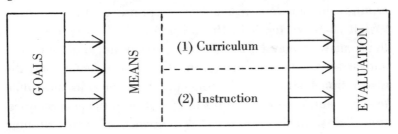

Figure 6. *The dynamic cycle of schooling.*

conditions for schools. In the figure the goals lead to the selection of means to be used in achieving those goals. Two classes of means are indicated for schools. One of them is a curriculum; the other is instruction that takes place in response to the curriculum. The processes of evaluation help us to determine the adequacy of the two means in producing the desired results — the achievement of the goals, and the results of evaluation help us to re-define the goals and replan the means for achieving them. Thus, a dynamic cycle is established for schooling.

This kind of reasoning, however, immediately indicates two geographic areas labeled as curriculum and instruction, and this very designation of curriculum and instruction as two categories instead of one is another source of confusion. Related to these are the purposes of having a curriculum in the first place, and it is here that the theorist must bring the relationships between curriculum and instruction into focus. What the contents of a curriculum are depends entirely upon whether both curriculum strategy and instructional strategy are to be encompassed in the curriculum design, and there does not seem to be any way of avoiding this decision. For investigators to theorize and conduct relevant research, their language and constructs have to be carefully ordered. It is rational for the two means of achieving the ends of schooling to be conceived as two sets of strategy. They are closely related, but are two sets nonetheless. One set is conceptualized around the answers reached in response to the question, "What shall we teach in the school(s)?" The expression of those answers may be termed the curriculum, and their form and arrangement the curriculum design. The second set, the instructional strategies, is conceptualized around individual teachers and groups of pupils in response to the general question, "How shall we teach?" A sequence of events running from the development of curriculum strategy, to the instructional strategy, to the actual activities of pupils in classrooms or elsewhere is thus a logical one. None of these strategies is pupil learnings. These rather take place as a result of the strategies. In fact, curriculum designers should plan strategies only in anticipation of learning activities and outcomes. In contrast, curriculum theorists or workers who think of curriculum strategy, instructional strategy, and/or actual classroom activities as constituting a single ball of wax called curriculum, pose an entirely different problem in curriculum design. Curriculum and schooling become almost the same concept. Curriculum design then includes an arrangement of objectives, subject matter chosen, specific action plans for teaching, all forms of instructional materials to be used, time schedules, activity descriptions, and so forth. If one goes further and includes what pupils learn as part of curriculum, the many components of evaluation also have to be added. In fact, it is difficult for the writer to conceptualize what a curriculum design would look like in such a scheme.

Document Features

For the remainder of this discussion of the contents of a curriculum, it is assumed that a curriculum is a written document. In this frame of reference, design features, or curriculum content and arrangement, are easily envisioned. A most commonly included feature is an outline of the subject matters to be taught. These statements, whether long or brief, usually are arranged sequentially by grades, or levels, according to the administrative organization of the school for which the curriculum is intended. A subsequent section of this chapter will be devoted entirely to this topic; thus here it will be left as one of the ingredients of a curriculum albeit a major one.

Another component that is frequently included in a curriculum is a statement of goals and/or specific objectives. These may range from statements of overall purpose of a school to very highly specific cognitive, psycho-motor, and affective changes in behavior sought through the efforts of a school. The same curriculum may contain a generalized statement of purposes for schooling in an introductory section and specific objectives in a second section in which the subject matters are described. One can find curriculums that contain only a statement of outcomes. The position taken by Johnson, cited in Chapter 4, would foster essentially this idea.[12] It will be recalled that to Johnson a curriculum is a set of intended learning outcomes. Johnson would include in the curriculum, in addition to the intended learning outcomes, rules for moving from the set of intended outcomes into the instructional domain, but he would relegate the choice of and organization of subject matters to those who are to develop the instructional strategies, rather than to those who are to plan the curriculum.

A third ingredient that may be included in a curriculum is a statement that sets forth the purposes for the creation of the curriculum and that stipulates the ways in which the curriculum is to be used. The most obvious need is for designers to state in straightforward language the relationships between the curriculum and the development of instructional strategies. The general process of moving from the planned curriculum to instruction is called curriculum implementation. Such statements in a curriculum may be thought of as a set of rules for implementation. Another possibility for inclusion would be a description of the contents and organization of the curriculum and the purposes for including each. A statement about the way in which the curriculum was planned, and how it is to be appraised and reconstructed, is generally warranted. The statement has most value as an early part in the curriculum. It facilitates the system of curriculum engineering for focalizing it.

A fourth possible item for inclusion in a curriculum, and and one that is rarely included, is an appraisal scheme. The appraisal scheme is a plan for determining the adequacy and worth of the curriculum and for identifying the intended contribution of the various parts to it. For example, if the

[12]Mauritz Johnson, Jr., "Definitions and Models in Curriculum Theory," *Educational Theory*, 17:127-140. April, 1967.

curriculum is intended to be used as a point of departure for all teachers in the development of their instructional strategies, whether or not they use it, and how well they use the curriculum for these purposes is the first place to bring the appraisal processes to bear. Another possibility is to test, through the appraisal scheme, any correlation between intended learning outcomes and learnings actually measured or observed subsequent to instruction. Since an appraisal scheme by definition furnishes data about the success and worth of the curriculum, the data becomes feedback information for reconstituting the curriculum contents and usage.

These four items appear to be reasonable for inclusion as parts of a curriculum. All curriculums include at least one of them. There may be other items that should be included, but they probably would fall under the general umbrella of one or more of these four. The next section contains a broadened description of issues in connection with the organization of subject matters. Most of the contemporary discussion about curriculum design falls under the general heading of subject matter organization, or the organization of the guides for instruction.

ORGANIZING AN INSTRUCTIONAL GUIDE

An instructional guide is that portion of a curriculum within which the subject matter selected to carry out the goals of schooling are contained. A word here is in order about the meanings associated with the phrase "subject matter." As used herein, subject matter embraces whatever is to be taught in the school: in school subjects, in selected disciplines, in problems of living, or in a pattern organized in any other way. Whatever the mode of expression, the subject matter is the substantive hard core of the curriculum. As discussed earlier, curriculum planners may choose not to include as part of a curriculum design the subject matters to be taught. In this case, the choice and organization of the subject matters would be delegated to the designers of instructional strategy. The issues and problems discussed in this section are thus relevant only in those cases where curriculum planners choose to include some design of subject matters or when curriculum planning and instructional-strategy planning are considered one and the same thing.

Organizational Patterns

Historically, variations in curriculum design have been identified with the ways of organizing subject matters. Most curriculum books contain some reference to types of curriculum that acquired their names from their design characteristics. All will be familiar with such displays in the language of the separate-subjects curriculum, the correlated curriculum, the broad fields curriculum, the activity curriculum, the problems of living curriculum, the persistent life situations curriculum, the core curriculum, the experience curriculum, the emergent curriculum. Supposedly, each of these called for a different design of the subject matter. It is fair to say that most of these tended to move away from a separate subjects approach toward a pattern believed to facilitate learning on the part of pupils. The fundamental argument was over the logical versus the psychological organization of subject matter. On the one hand, proponents of logical organization contended that school subjects had their own internal organization and that curriculum planners should create curriculum designs that would capitalize upon the logical orderliness of the subjects. Advocates of psychological organization of subject matter emphaized an organization allegedly designed to facilitate learning by pupils because the organization aided pupils in the integration of subject matters from several or all of the school subjects.

All are familiar with the great revival of interest in curriculum beginning around mid-century. The combined effect of critics of school practices, the availability of foundational and governmental grants of money for the study of education, and an upsurge of interest in problems of curriculum and instruction by scholars from the various disciplines produced a rash of curriculum activity. The projects on high school physics and biology and the elementary school programs in mathematics and foreign languages are illustrative.

It is most interesting to note that in the more recent developments, the direction of change is directly opposite that of the earlier period. In the earlier period, attempts were made to move away from a separate-subjects scheme of organization toward an organization in which the individual subjects would lose their separate identities by being combined, for instance, into language arts, social studies, core, persistent life situation, or problems of living designs. The more recent innovations stress a return to the organizational features of the individual disciplines and to more careful programing of each discipline according to its own characteristics and rules. Furthermore, most of the newly developed designs have been characterized as curriculum innovations even though they are concerned exclusively with single subjects, such as mathematics, chemistry, or English. Little, or no, attention is given to the interrelationships among the various subjects, nor do the designers give evidence of realizing that a curriculum is something that has to characterize a whole school program.

School organization has a great deal of influence upon the design features of curriculum also. It is easier to talk about the whole curriculum, or the fusion of subjects, in elementary schools where the organizational pattern is the self-contained classroom than in the departmentalized multi-teacher organization of the secondary schools. Many of our preconceived notions about curriculum design may have to change drastically under the stimulation of such features as team teaching and nongraded units. But one cannot help wondering which comes first — administrative organizational patterns like nongradedness and modular scheduling or a curulum design. Textbooks on professional education boldly state that we first must decide upon what kind of curriculum we wish to carry out in our schools before determining a pattern or organization for the school. So far, differences between a curriculum designed for a graded school and a nongraded school are few in number; customarily, portions of the same curriculum are assigned to the variously constituted groups. Irrespective of this state of affairs, it is important to note that a principle in curriculum design is that the design and the organizational scheme of any school need to be in harmony.

Content versus Process

There persists an argument about the relative merits of a content-centered approach to organization of subject matter and a process-centered approach. For the curriculum theorists, this appears to be an argument that warrants considerable attention. What adds to the confusion is that writers assign various meanings to the terms "content" and "process," and the theorist is confronted with a problem of selecting definitions of technical terms. Some of these meanings will illustrate the complexity of the problem.

The original dichotomization of the terms content and process probably originated over arguments about whether teachers should be predominantly concerned with the content to be learned by pupils or with the processes of learning used by the pupils. Although, in actual fact, the answer never is one or the other, the argument arose as a result of the shifting of emphasis from content to be learned to the learning processes — the latter an area that dominated professional effort during the 1920's and the 1930's. A second distinction was made between the content of a subject and the processes of applying elements of content to the solution of social and practical problems. Here again, we can see that no real choice exists for the curriculum planner. Recently, there has been much discussion about the content of the disciplines and the modes of inquiry associated with them. We will highlight more of this argument in the subsequent discussion of the disciplines and their structures as bases for organizing guides for instruction.

An interesting position has been taken by Parker and Rubin that tends to dissolve the problem of content and process conceived as a dichotomy.[13] They contend that process should be interpreted as content in curriculum designing. They cite the following four tasks for the curriculum worker:

> 1. *A retooling of subject matter to illuminate base structure, and to insure that knowledge which generates knowledge takes priority over knowledge which does not;*
> 2. *An examination of the working methods of the intelectual practitioner: the biologist, the historian, the political scientist, for the significant processes of their craft, and the use of these processes in our classroom instruction;*
> 3. *The utilization of the evidence gathered from a penetrating study of people doing things, as they go about the business of life, in reordering the curriculum;*
> 4. *A deliberate effort to school the child in the conditions for cross-application of the processes he has mastered — the ways and means of putting them to good use elsewhere.*[14]

[13]J. Cecil Parker and Louis J. Rubin, *Process as Content: Curriculum Design and the Application of Knowledge* (Chicago: Rand McNally and Company, 1966).

[14]*Ibid.*, p. 48.

Disciplines and Their Structures

Another task for the curriculum theorist as he seeks better explanations for the organization of subject matters is to determine the nature of the disciplines and their structures, and assess their curriculum implications. There has been a plethora of publications in recent years advancing the proposition that curriculum content should be organized around the established disciplines. These publications have been reviewed again and again in such journals as the *Review of Educational Research* and in numerous books and pamphlets; thus there is no need for a further review of them here. A number of references are cited at the end of this chapter for those who wish to delve into the details. Our purpose here exclusively is to assess the implications of the issue for curriculum design.

A discipline generally is thought to be a branch of knowledge that is organized so as to facilitate its instruction and its development. It consists of a related series of concepts and principles which constitute the domain of the discipline. This is the content, or organized knowledge, generated by those who have worked in the discipline. A discipline has characteristic ways of behavior for the solution of problems. A discipline has a history, or a tradition, accumulated in the process of generating knowledge and developing unique ways of solving problems. Obviously, it is impossible to think of a discipline without considering the persons who choose to work in the discipline as part of it; they are the disciples.

In his analysis of the structures of disciplines, Schwab identified three basic problem areas: the organization of a discipline, the substantive structures of a discipline, and the syntactical structures of a discipline.[15] The organization of a

[15]Joseph J. Schwab, "Problems, Topics, and Issues," *Education and the Structure of Knowledge*, Stanley Elam, editor (Chicago: Rand McNally and Company, 1964), pp. 4-43.

discipline refers to its orientation with respect to other disciplines. Orientation is helpful in currciulum organization in determining which discipline areas may be joined together and which need to remain separate. The substantive structure of a discipline refers to the knowledge produced by the discipline. For curriculum design, the substantive structure may be interpreted as that part of the content needed to be understood by pupils. Syntactical structure of a discipline refers to the modes and rules for generating proof or new knowledge. Ways in which scholars in the various disciplines gather and evaluate data, pose their hypotheses, and assert their generalizations are receiving a great deal of current attention as part of curriculum content.

The main thesis of those who have pushed for "discipline-centerdness" in curriculum design is that knowledge contained in the disciplines, and only in the disciplines, belongs in a school's curriculum. Phenix stated it in this way:

> My thesis, briefly, is that *all* curriculum content should be drawn from the disciplines, or, to put it another way, that *only* knowledge contained in the disciplines is appropriate to the curriculum.[16]

King and Brownell accept the same thesis as Phenix when they postulate that only those who are qualified members of the discipline group of scholars should participate in curriculum planning.[17] Thus they would eliminate all non-discipline knowledge from a curriculum.

The problem of sequence is solved by the selection of topics from the organized disciplines and the spiraling of them in terms of difficulty for various age groups. Bruner stated the hypothesis: "that any subject can be taught effec-

[16]Philip H. Phenix, "The Disciplines as Curriculum Content," *Curriculum Crossroads*, A. Harry Passow, editor, New York: Bureau of Publications, Teachers College, Columbia University, 1962), p. 57.

[17]Arthur R. King, Jr. and John A. Brownell, *The Curriculum and the Disciplines of Knowledge* (New York: John Wiley and Sons, Inc., 1966).

tively in some intellectually honest form to any child at any stage of development."[18] He proposed a spiral curriculum graduated in difficulty from the elementary to the complex. It is important to note that the criteria for selection, scope, and sequence as curriculum design features are all based upon the inherent worth of the knowledge and the modes of inquiry characteristic of the disciplines.

A special case of the application of discipline-centeredness to curriculum design is exhibited by those who are creating programed materials for instruction. Two cases will illustrate, both in mathematics. One is the work being carried on by Patrick Suppes at Stanford University on computerized instruction in mathematics. Suppes has been developing carefully programed sequences for the development of concepts and the ability to solve problems in which children must apply those concepts. The use of the computer in instruction provides for individualized instruction. The computer-based teaching machines provide immediate feedback and corrective measures when necessary.

A second illustration is the University of Maryland Mathematics Project. In this program each learning step is programed so that a hierarchical sequence of "learning sets" results. Positive transfer is assumed from one level to a higher level of learning set. Exercises for pupils are provided, and appropriate achievement tests administered.

There are two reasons for efforts like these to be considered as special cases in curriculum design. One is the careful programing of content. The other is that programs of this kind not only create curriculum answers to the question of what should be taught in schools; they also provide the instructional strategies and modes of appraisal. In this sense they are unitary packages designed to solve the many problems of schooling.

[18]Jerome S. Bruner, *The Process of Education* (Cambridge: Harvard University Press, 1961), p. 33.

Form and Arrangement

Any concept of curriculum design must account for the form and arrangement of subject matter. Under a discipline-centered, or a subject-centered, scheme, each of the subjects is arranged sequentially so that the various sub-topics fit the vertical organization of the school; however, interrelationships among the chosen subjects, or disciplines, tend to be ignored. Bellack stated the problem as follows:

> When one looks beyond the structure of the individual disciplines and asks about the structure of the curriculum, attention is focused on *relationships* among the various fields that comprise the program of studies. For just as relationships among ideas is at the heart of the concept of structure as applied to the individual disciplines, so relationships among the disciplines is at the heart of the notion of structure as applied to the curriculum as a whole.[19]

At the heart of this problem is the quest for better explanations in respect to the selection of subject matter ingredients. Presumably, one selects subject matter that will fulfill the goals set for education in schools. If it is possible to be convinced that the goals for schooling are achievable by curriculum designers organizing the total subject matter into discrete disciplines, or subjects, then it is reasonable to expect goal fulfillment to be directed by such design. On the other hand, if the goals set for schooling call for planned interrelationships among the various disciplines, or subjects, it is unreasonable to predict their achievement from a design composed of discretely organized components. Very few would argue that knowledge taken from disciplines and their structures is not important for the school curriculum, but many would take the position, as did Bellack, that curriculum de-

[19] Arno A. Bellack, "The Structure of Knowledge and the Structure of the Curriculum," *A Reassessment of the Curriculum.* Dwayne Huebner, editor (New York: Bureau of Publications, Teachers College, Columbia University, 1964), p. 28.

sign is more complicated.

The complex nature of educational goals makes the task of form and arrangement of subject matter difficult. Goals may be classified into four categories. The first, a cognitive one, includes the basic concepts of knowledge, key ideas, generalizations, principles, and laws. It is in response to this goal category that school curriculums have provided content to be learned. A second category consists of modes of inquiry for solving problems in the areas of organized knowledge such as observation, classification, inference, and prediction. It also includes the psycho-motor skills of communication. A third category of goal consists of the development of affective behaviors. This is the domain of values, emotions, attitudes, and appreciations. A fourth category includes the development of abilities to make applications of learning to social and personal problems of living, particularly problems demanding that knowledge and skills developed in several subjects be brought to bear. A curriculum for today's schools must serve all of these. They have been talked about extensively, but little has been done to fulfill all of them. The task is a very great challenge for those who address themselves to curriculum design.

What we are talking about in this section is the design features or organization of subject matter. This section of a curriculum is more closely related to the instructional strategies to follow than any other section. However, it is the form and the arrangement of the subject matter that is most often discussed under curriculum design or patterns of curriculum organization. So far, we have discussed some of the historical arrangements and the recent accent upon discipline-centeredness. Possibilities for arrangement of the total subject matter need to be added to the discussion.

In this connection, Goodlad has proposed the use of organizing centers and organizing elements as bases for curriculum organization.[20] Organizing centers represent the form in which subject matter is organized: for example, a textbook, a problem, an experiment, a resource unit, or a broad field of study. Organizing elements, on the other hand, refer to a classification of anticipated learnings such as concepts, generalizations, skills, values, attitudes, or modes of inquiry. The idea of building a curriculum around organizing centers and organizing elements is a way of attacking problems posed by the complex goals of schooling.

Goodlad's position is similar to the Tyler rationale. Tyler identified as organizing elements for a curriculum the concepts, skills, and values cited as behavioral objectives for pupils. Specific subjects, broad fields, core lessons, topics, or units he referred to as organizing structures. Organizing principles called for use of chronological order, extension outward from pupils' lives, the use of concrete materials and ideas prior to abstraction, and increasing the breadth and application of knowledge.[21]

Beauchamp has proposed a device intended to be used for purposes of constructing the instructional guide as one of the components of a curriculum. It is illustrated in Figure 7.

The functions of the worksheet illustrated in Figure 7 are self-evident. The first column provides opportunity to arrange topics, social problems, units, or specific elements of a subject. The arrangement in this column should demonstrate the scope of the content selected to carry out the school's overall goals. This arrangement would correspond roughly with Goodlad's organizing centers. The second column is included as a means of suggesting to those who will use the

[20]John I. Goodlad, *Planning and Organizing for Teaching* (Washington: Project on the Instructional Program of the Public Schools, NEA, 1963). pp. 42-47.

[21]Ralph W. Tyler, "Curriculum Organization," *The Integration of Educational Experiences,* Fifty-seventh Yearbook, National Society for the Study of Education, Part III (Chicago: The University of Chicago Press, 1958), pp. 105-125.

INSTRUCTIONAL GUIDE

Subject or Unit _____

Grade _____

Subject Matter Breakdown in Topics or Units	Suggested Activities For Children to Perform	Expected Outcomes in Changed Pupil Behavior		
		Concepts, Facts or Generalizations to Be Learned	Skill Performances to Be Developed	Developmental Values to Be Acquired

Figure 7. *An instructional guide worksheet.*

curriculum as a point of departure for developing instructional strategies what general kinds of things the curriculum planners anticipated in selecting the content. This column should be brief and suggestive only. Some would prefer to eliminate this use and substitute for it suggestions for needed instructional materials. Again this would be suggestive only because such matters more appropriately are a part of the development of instructional strategies. The third column is intended to reveal the kinds of behavioral outcomes the curriculum planners predict for pupils. The column is subdivided into three classes of behavioral outcomes. One class consists of the concepts, generalizations, and laws to be learned. These make up the cognitive behaviors. Another consists of proficiencies in inquiry and all of the psycho-motor skills. The third is "developmental values." Entries under it reflect behavior aspirations in the realm of values, attitudes, appreciation, compassion, and so forth. The behavioral outcomes roughly correspond to Goodlad's organizing elements. The proper use of Figure 7 helps, because of its design characteristics, to arrange subject matter in a form that gives a set of checks and balances on directions for achieving all four of the types of goal for schooling that were discussed earlier. It is just one design illustration; creative minds should be able to come up with others that serve similar purposes.

An illustration of a third type of design for the subject matter section of a curriculum is that conceived and advocated by Stratemeyer, et. al.[22] This particular design is based upon the concept of persistent life situations. Persistent life situations are defined as "those situations that recur in the life of the individual in many different ways as he grows from infancy to maturity."[23] The major areas within

[22]Florence B. Stratemeyer, Hamden L. Forkner, Margaret G. McKim, and A. Harry Passow, *Developing A Curriculum for Modern Living* (second edition; New York: Bureau of Publications, Teachers College, Columbia University, 1957).

[23]*Ibid.*, p. 45.

which persistent life situations are found are health, intellectual power, moral choices, aesthetic expression and appreciation, person-to-person relationships, group membership, intergroup relationships, natural phenomena, technological resources, and economic-social-political structures and forces. Within each of the major areas, specific persistent life situations are identified. For example, under the major area "intellectual power," Stratemeyer includes making oral presentations, expressing ideas in written form, using graphic forms to express ideas, using source materials, understanding symbols and relationships, budgeting time and energy, and solving practical problems that persistently recur.[24] Individuals face situations like these in more or less complicated form depending upon their level of growth and maturity; thus curriculum design must account for them. The reader will observe that a design of the persistent life situations type is drastically different from a design that employs disciplines and their structures as a fundamental point of departure. The same may be said of core, broad-fields, or social problems as basic orientations. The discipline-centered approach proceeds from the logical organization of selected portions of the disciplines which themselves are logically organized. The persistent life situations type proceeds from perceived social, cultural, and personal needs of the school pupils. In this sense, they are psychologically oriented.

Yet another proposal, and the last to be identified here, for the form and arrangement of subject matter is that elaborated by Broudy, Smith, and Burnett.[25] It should be noted first that Broudy, Smith, and Burnett believe that the secondary school should be an institution to provide for the

[24]*Ibid.* pp. 155-165.

[25]Harry S. Broudy, B. Othanel Smith, and Joe R. Burnett, *Democracy and Excellence in American Secondary Education* (Chicago: Rand McNally and Company, 1964).

general education of the adolescent population. They reject the notion of terminal, or vocational education as the responsibility of the secondary school. The pros and cons of of this argument obviously cannot be given here in detail, but the point is essential to an understanding of the design proposal.

For Broudy, Smith, and Burnett, curriculum consists primarily of two elements. One of the elements is content which is characterized by facts, descriptive and valuative concepts, principles, and norms and rules. The other element consists of categories of instruction organized under symbolic studies, basic sciences, developmental studies, aesthetic studies, and molar problems.[26] The specific design features of this proposal are illustrated in Figure 8. Certainly, this design is radically different from the usual array of required and elective courses that is traditional with our secondary schools.

TRENDS IN PRACTICE

What goes on in practice is a convenient way for anyone to analyze curriculum design characteristics. One may review either content of curriculum or of curriculum guides. Merritt and Harap did a thorough job of this in 1955.[27] A repeat of this study is needed to give a picture of the present state of affairs; however, a reasonable assumption is that most of the physical characteristics reported by Merritt and Harap are still evident in curriculums of today's schools.

Recognizing this need, a group of graduate students under

[26]*Ibid.*, pp. 78-83.

[27]Eleanor Merritt and Henry Harap, *Trends in the Production of Curriculum Guides* (Nashville: Divivion of Surveys and Field Services, George Peabody College for Teachers, 1955).

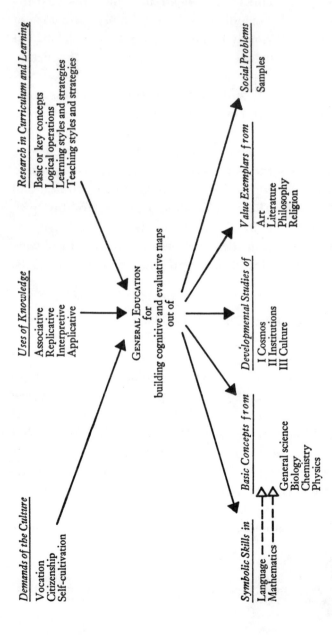

Figure 8. *Design for common curriculum in general education (grades 7-12).* Adapted by permission from Harry S. Broudy, B. Othanel Smith, and Joe R. Burnett, *Democracy and Excellence in American Secondary Education* (Chicago: Rand McNally and Company, 1964), p. 160.

the writer's urging analyzed a sample of recent curriculums for elementary and secondary schools.[28] Most curriculums reviewed included a statement of objectives. Little relationship was customarily found to exist between many of the statements of objectives and the materials that followed those statements. This finding agrees with the ones of Merritt and Harap in 1955.

Most curriculums include instructional guides. They generally are organized by subject. In them, more instructions are given customarily to teachers in elementary curriculums than in secondary ones. This seems to constitute a vote of greater faith in the instructional ingenuity of the secondary school teacher than of the elementary teacher. Irrespective of this issue, there is great variation in size of instructional guides as indicated by the number of pages devoted to a subject as well as by the content on the pages. There is a trend toward detailing the entries so as to solve instructional problems. The trend is reflected in the amount of attention given to instructional materials and teaching strategies. More of this kind of detail is present when instructional guides are published by subject rather than as general guides. Curriculum offices in large city school systems tend to prepare larger volumes than the smaller school districts.

Rarely do curriculums contain evaluation schemes or specific implementation instructions. The former probably reflects our artlessness about evaluation in general and about curriculum in particular. Lack of specific implementation instructions may mean that they are provided by some other means such as administrative dictum. It may be a reflection of fear of imposing too rigidly upon the rights of teachers to decide their own teaching strategies.

[28] I am indebted to Lois Lind, Marshall Lind, and Michael Hinkemeyer for undertaking this task.

SUMMARY

The way to communicate about the meanings associated with a curriculum is to talk about curriculum design. To describe design features is a mode of defining a curriculum. The essential dimensions of curriculum design discussed in this chapter may be graphically displayed in a model for curriculum design. A suggested one is shown in Figure 9.

It is axiomatic to the writer that anyone who talks about a curriculum needs first to conceive it as a written document. If Figure 9 is used as a design model, the resulting curriculum would contain four sections: (1) a statement of purposes, (2) an instructional guide that displays behavioral objectives and content organization in harmony with school organization, (3) a set of guidelines (or rules) governing the use of the curriculum, and (4) an evaluation scheme. The model thus provides for most of the demands placed upon a curriculum. A curriculum, for instance, should be so designed that teachers can and will use it as a point of departure for developing their teaching strategies. All dimensions of the model contribute to this need for a curriculum. A curriculum should be designed to fit the organizational pattern of the school for which it is intended. In Figure 9, this demand is satisfied by calling for recognition of school organization upon which content and objectives are imposed. Names of levels 1, 2, 3, and 4 in the model have deliberately been withheld so that the model may be fitted to any school organization scheme: grades, modules, achievement levels, sections, or any other title.

The most controversial issue of curriculum design is the treatment to be given to subject matter. The scope differentially embraces statements of objectives, elaborate displays of topics, behavioral objectives, pupil activities, instructional

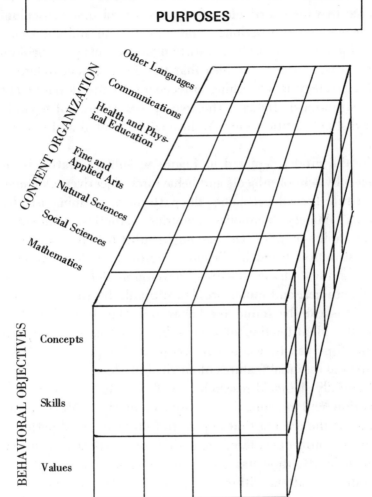

Figure 9. *A model for curriculum design.*

materials, and time allotments. At the root of this issue is the degree to which curriculum designers intend that curriculum strategies and instructional strategies be one and the same. The dilemma here resides in unwillingness of many curriculum strategists to accept the idea that the development of curriculum strategy is something antecedent to the development of instructional strategy. The two, however, are not separate and distinct entities; they are intimately related and sequential.

In the model depicted in Figure 9, subject matter is arranged by school subjects and behavioral objectives. One may substitute for subject names the patterns of meaning used by Phenix, namely, symbolics, empirics, esthetics, synnoetics, ethics, and synoptics. Or, one might substitute the categories of instruction listed by Broudy, Smith, and Burnett: symbolic studies, basic sciences, developmental studies, aesthetic studies, and molar problems. Similarly, substitute designations can be found for behavioral objectives. Nonetheless, the identification of what subject matter and how it is to be displayed to account for scope and sequence are legitimate and essential features of curriculum design.

Carefully designed research is badly needed in the area of selection and organization of subject matters. Most curriculums at the present time appear to follow identical patterns. They are subject-centered, and they are vertically arranged. Too little attention has been paid to horizontal articulation of subject matters within schools and grades. If we ever are to capitalize upon the common, or greatly similar, elements in the various subjects, or disciplines, that we are to teach, something resembling fusion of subject matter will have to be refelcted in curriculum design.

SUGGESTED READINGS

Alberty, Harold B. and Elsie J. Alberty. *Reorganizing the High-School Curriculum.* Third edition. New York: The Macmillan Company, 1962.

Alexander, William M. *Changing Curriculum Content: Report of the Conference on Curriculum Content.* Washington: Association for Supervision and Curriculum Development, NEA, 1964.

Ammons, Margaret. "The Definition, Function, and Use of Educational Objectives," *The Elementary School Journal,* 62:432-436. May, 1962.

Anderson, Dan W., James B. Macdonald, and Frank B. May (eds.). *Strategies of Curriculum Development.* Columbus: Charles E.Merrill Books, 1965.

Beauchamp, George A. *The Curriculum of the Elementary School.* Boston: Allyn and Bacon, Inc., 1964.

Bloom, Benjamin S. (ed.). *Taxonomy of Educational Objectives: Handbook I Cognitive Domain.* New York: Longmans, Green and Company, 1956.

Broudy, Harry S., B. Othanel Smith, and Joe R. Burnett. *Democracy and Excellence in American Secondary Education.* Chicago: Rand McNally and Company, 1964.

Bruner, Jerome S. *The Process of Education.* Cambridge: Harvard University Press, 1961.

Educational Policies Commission. *The Central Purpose of American Education.* Washington: the Commission, 1961.

Elam, Stanley (ed.). *Education and the Structure of Knowledge.* Chicago: Rand McNally and Company, 1964.

Ford, G. W. and Lawrence Pugno (eds.). *The Structure of Knowledge and the Curriculum.* Chicago: Rand McNally and Company, 1964.

Foshay, Arthur W. "A Modest Proposal," *Educational Leadership* 18: 506-516, May, 1961.

Gilchrist, Robert S., Chairman. *Using Current Curriculum Developments.* Washington: Association for Supervision and Curriculum Development, NEA, 1963.

Goodlad, John I. *The Changing School Curriculum.* New York: Fund for the Advancement of Education, 1966.

Heath, Robert W. (ed.). *New Curricula.* New York: Harper and Row, 1964.

Huebner, Dwayne (ed.). *A Reassessment of the Curriculum.* New York: Bureau of Publications, Teachers College, Columbia University, 1964.

Hughes, Philip. "Decisions and Curriculum Design," *Educational Theory*, 12:187-192, July, 1962.

Inlow, Gail M. *The Emergent in Curriculum.* New York: John Wiley and Sons, Inc., 1966.

Johnson, Mauritz, Jr. "Definitions and Models in Curriculum Theory," *Educational Theory*, 17:127-140, April, 1967.

Kearney, Nolan C. *Elementary School Objectives: A Report Prepared for the Mid-Century Committee on Outcomes in Elementary Education.* New York: Russell Sage Foundation, 1953.

King, Arthur R. and John A. Brownell. *The Curriculum and the Disciplines of Knowledge.* New York: John Wiley and Sons, Inc., 1966.

Krathwohl, David R., Benjamin S. Bloom, and Bertram B. Masia. *Taxonomy of Educational Objectives: Handbook II Affective Domain.* New York: David McKay Company, Inc., 1964.

Krug, Edward A. *Curriculum Planning.* Revised edition. New York: Harper and Row, 1957.

Merritt, Eleanor and Henry Harap. *Trends in the Production of Curriculum Guides.* Nashville: Division of Surveys and Field Services, George Peabody College for Teachers, 1955.

Parker, Cecil J. and Louis J. Rubin. *Process as Content: Curriculum Design and the Application of Knowledge.* Chicago: Rand McNally and Company, 1966.

Passow, A. Harry (ed.). *Curriculum Crossroads.* New York: Bureau of Publications, Teachers College, Columbia University, 1962.

Phenix, Philip H. *Realms of Meaning.* New York: McGraw-Hill Book Company, 1964.

Ragan, William B. *Modern Elementary Curriculum.* Third edition. New York: Holt, Rinehart, and Winston, Inc., 1966.

Smith, B. Othanel, William O. Stanley, and J. Harlan Shores. *Fundamentals of Curriculum Development.* Revised edition. Yonkers-on-Hudson: World Book Company, 1957.

Stratemeyer, Florence B., Hamden L. Forkner, Margaret G. McKim, and A. Harry Passow. *Developing a Curriculum for Modern Living.* Second edition. New York: Bureau of Publications, Teachers College, Columbia University, 1957.

Taba, Hilda. *Curriculum Development: Theory and Practice.* New York: Harcourt, Brace and World, Inc., 1962.

Taylor, Philip H. *Purpose and Structure in the Curriculum.* An Inaugural Lecture Delivered in the University of Birmingham, England on November 3, 1966.

Tyler, Ralph, W. "Curriculum Organization," *The Integration of Educational Experiences.* Fifty-seventh Yearbook of the National Society for the Study of Education, Part III, 1958, pp. 105-125.

Unruh, Glenys G. (ed.). *New Curriculum Developments.* Washington: Association for Supervision and Curriculum Development, NEA. 1965.

6

CURRICULUM

ENGINEERING

A curriculum system is a system for both decision-making and action with respect to curriculum functions regarded as a part of the total operations of schooling. The system has three primary functions: (1) to produce a curriculum, (2) to implement the curriculum, and (3) to appraise the effectiveness of the curriculum and the curriculum system. The primary ingredient in effectuating these functions is decision-making by the persons involved, and the decision-making tasks are complicated both by the nature of the tasks and the number of persons involved. The complications call for intelligent human engineering if the functions are to be carried out effectively. Hence, the title *Curriculum Engineering* is used to represent both the system and its internal dynamics.

Curriculum engineering consists of all of the processes necessary to make a curriculum system functional in schools.

The chief engineers in the curriculum system are the superintendent of schools, principals, and curriculum directors, and they may be assisted by consultative personnel from outside the school system. They, the engineers, organize and direct the manipulation of the various tasks and operations that must go on in order for a curriculum to be planned, implemented in classrooms through the instructional program, evaluated, and revised in light of the data accumulated through evaluation. Thus, curriculum engineering encompasses the set of activities necessary to keep the curriculum of a school in a dynamic state.

In this chapter, the scope of curriculum engineering activities will be identified by pointing up the critical areas of concern in any curriculum system and by noting alternative choices leading to different theoretical positions. Before turning to these critical choices, it is necessary for us to describe more carefully than we have done so far the precise character of the more important systems of schooling, and the characteristics of a curriculum system.

SYSTEMS OF SCHOOLING

A convenient way for theorists and practitioners to identify a curriculum system and its prescribed roles is to observe its place among other systems of schooling. By schooling is meant all those activities essential to the purposeful maintenance and operation of schools. The systems of schooling are operational constructs that explain the character of schooling, and that have identifiable characteristics internally. These can be represented diagrammatically, one such diagram being included here as Figure 10. In it, the language of set relationships is used to explain the interrela-

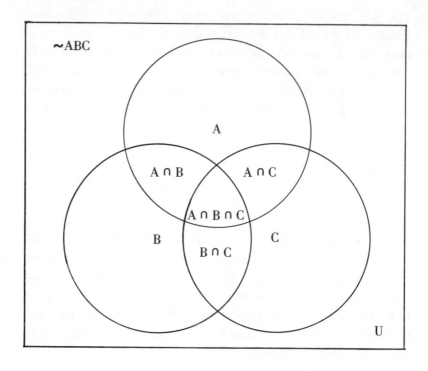

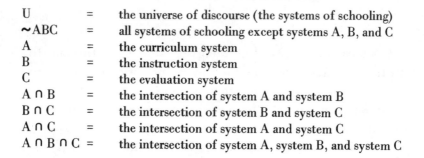

Legend:

U	=	the universe of discourse (the systems of schooling)
~ABC	=	all systems of schooling except systems A, B, and C
A	=	the curriculum system
B	=	the instruction system
C	=	the evaluation system
A ∩ B	=	the intersection of system A and system B
B ∩ C	=	the intersection of system B and system C
A ∩ C	=	the intersection of system A and system C
A ∩ B ∩ C =		the intersection of system A, system B, and system C

Figure 10. *A diagram representing the systems of schooling.*

tionships among the various systems of schooling. The symbol U designates the universal set, or universe of discourse, which represents schooling. Subset A represents the curriculum system. Subset B represents the instructional system, and subset C represents the evaluation system. Subset ABC represents all subsets, or systems, of schooling not included in A, B, and C; in this case, curriculum, instruction, and evaluation. To these might be added the administrative system, the personnel services system, the guidance system, and so forth. Our major concern here is with the three systems curriculum, instruction, and evaluation because they more nearly characterize the fundamental nature of schooling than any others.

The set interesctions shown in Figure 10 are very interesting. They represent the interactions of two or more of the three systems. This interaction, or overlay, of the systems graphically portrays the continuity among curriculum, instruction, and evaluation. It helps to establish that there are no discrete boundaries among systems, and that systems have purposes in common. For example, the intersection of curriculum and instruction might represent such functions as planning for implementation, lesson planning, and teacher-pupil planning. These functions bridge the gap between decisions about what to teach and decisions about how to teach. The intersection of curriculum and evaluation might represent the evaluation of the degree of curriculum implementation, evaluation of teacher use of the curriculum, evaluation of curriculum organization, or feedback of information from evaluation for curriculum revision. These functions bridge the gap between the decisions made about what to teach and the judgments made about the predictability and the worth of those decisions. The intersection of instruction and evaluation represents the functions that bridge the gap between activities associated with the execution of decisions about how to teach and appraisal of those activities via such means as diagnostic testing by the teacher, pupil self-evaluations, appraisal of teaching preformances, or the evaluation of instructional materials. The intersection of all three systems is the payoff area of schooling. This intersection represents pupil learnings as planned for in the curriculum system, as taught for in the instruction system, and as tested or observed in the evaluation system. All systems point toward pupil learnings. All systems make some contribution to pupil learnings.

THE CURRICULUM SYSTEM

The general purpose of a curriculum system as one of the several systems of schooling is to provide a framework for deciding what shall be taught in the schools and for employing those decisions as points of departure for developing instructional strategies. Every school and/or school district has one of these systems irrespective of whether it be visible or invisible, conscious or unconscious, organized or random. At some time, in some way, and by someone, a set of decisions has to be reached about what is to be taught to achieve the goals of the school. The system used to plan the curriculum, implement it, and appraise its effectiveness is the curriculum system.

The language of systems analysis is useful in describing the basic characteristics of a curriculum system. Figure 11 is a diagram of a model of a curriculum system using that language. The system is composed of three essential components: (1) a body of input data, (2) the necessary content and processes for the maintenance of the system, and (3) the output of the system. In Figure 11, the entries under each of the three

Input

Educational foundations
Community characteristics
Personalities of persons
  involved
Curriculum experience
The subject matters from
  disciplines and other
  subjects
Social and cultural values

**Content and Processes for
System Maintenance**

Choice of arena for curriculum
  processes
Selection of personnel
Selection and execution of working
  procedures for:
    determining curricular goals
    selection of curriculum design
    planning and writing
Establishing implementation procedures
Establishing procedures for appraising
  and revising the curriculum

Output

A curriculum
Increased knowledge
  by participants
Changed attitudes
Commitment to act

Figure 11. *A model of a curriculum system.*

components are brief and generalized to avoid contamination by any specific position with respect to curriculum engineering. The purpose here is to illustrate what a system is and how it works regardless of specific choices any individual or group might make within the general system framework.

Input Data

The function of input data is to provide energy for the content and processes that maintain the steady state of the system. Energy in this case is the intellectual and personal driving power engendered by such forces as educational foundations, relevant community characteristics, human personalities involved, experience of schools with curriculum affairs, the large body of human knowledge stored and categorized in the disciplines and other school subjects, and relevant social and cultural values. Input data constitute the sources of authority, or the sources of potential behaviors and content ideas, for the curriculum engineering that must take place at the level of system maintenance. During the system maintenance processes, relevant information, procedures, and values have to be selected from the input sources. This selection process is one of the reasons why working in a full curriculum system is educative for the participants.

Content and Processes for System Maintenance

Any system is characterized by a known body of activities that make the system work and maintain itself. Figure 11 lists the basic functions that must go on for a curriculum system to be maintained. We shall mention them only briefly here because they are the areas of substantial issue and controversy in curriculum. The principal choices among them will be discussed in detail in the next section of the chapter. There is sequential order to the way these functions are listed in Figure 11. A first choice that must be made by those in authority for schooling is the arena in which curriculum activities are to take place. The arena is where curriculum planning is to be done and implementation functions are to be directed. Once the arena choice has been made, the persons who are to be involved in curriculum decision-making may be chosen. Once the persons to be involved have been identified, working procedures may be planned to determine the curricular goals, to select a curriculum design, to develop details of the design, and actually to do the writing of the curriculum. Procedures will have to be planned to move from the curriculum system to the instructional system; these constitute the implementation plans. Finally, plans need to be made to appraise the output of the curriculum system and the data used to revise both curriculum and the activities of the curriculum system. All of these are warranted ingredients of what may be called a curriculum system.

Output

The most obvious and necessary output of a curriculum system is a planned curriculum, and it is the only visible output. Other outputs such as changed attitudes of teachers and other participants in the system, increased knowledge by the participants because the planning process has been educative, and a commitment by teachers and school leaders to implement and to appraise the curriculum are just as real as the planned curriculum, but they are not always visible.

Schools have a long history of curriculum planning, but not many have examined the outputs of those efforts. Even more important, curriculum practitioners have had little experience in using the results of examining curriculum outputs as feedback data to improve futher curriculum efforts. To appraise the magnitude of these outputs, measures that will identify the traits involved and the magnitude of them will have to be constructed. The development of instruments that would give us these measures needs to be among the next steps of curriculum research.

THEORETICAL ISSUES

The curriculum theorist finds more immediate food for his efforts in systems of curriculum engineering than in any other area of the total field of curriculum. The most plausible reason for this is the vast experience we have had in this country with curriculum planning. It is true that our experience with the task and method variables of curriculum implementation and curriculum evaluation has been limited; the reason is because we have not worked hard at these dimensions. But we have worked hard at the tasks and methods of curriculum planning. The alternative ways of accomplishing the various tasks of curriculum engineering provide the theorist with a basic classification scheme from which the beginning elements of curriculum theories may be deduced, and from which further research may be launched to develop additional generalizations. Most, if not all, of the general areas of curriculum engineering that serve as basic structure to this kind of classification have been indicated in Figure 11 under the content and processes for system maintenance. We now turn to each of them.

The Arena for Curriculum Engineering

The first decision that has to be reached in establishing a

system for curriculum engineering is the arena in which the various curriculum activities are to take place and to be directed. Most subsequent choices are to some degree dependent upon the choice of arena; therefore, it is not a choice to be taken lightly.

Moving from smaller to larger, the most obvious arena choices are the individual school, the school district, the state, and the nation. In the United States, education legally has been a function of the several states. In turn, most state governments have delegated operational control to the various school districts. It has been this act that has resulted in so much autonomy being vested in the hands of local school district officials, including the development of curriculums for the schools. There are, of course, some cases in which state legislatures have passed laws insisting that certain subject matters be taught in schools of the state such as teaching about the state constitution, instruction about the evils of narcotics, or a given number of minutes per week to be devoted to physical education. In some states, state departments of education have created suggestive curriculum guides. But in the main, curriculum decisions have been left to authorities of local school districts. This phenomenon probably accounts for the fact that the most commonly used arena for curriculum planning in the United States is the school district. Occasionally, the authorities of a school district assign curriculum decision-making to individual schools. However, the quest for similarity, or uniformity, encourages district authorities to retain responsibility for, and control over, the functions. Until recent years writers and planners have given little thought to the nation as an arena for curriculum decision-making, but the situation is in the act of reversing itself today. As the federal government has invested more heavily in schooling and has expanded its services, individuals have proposed the nation as an arena.

It should be kept in mind that the choice of arena for curriculum engineering encompasses all of the activities (planning, implementation, and evaluation) inherent in a system of curriculum engineering, and the choice of arena has some effect upon all subsequent choices. For example, the problem of implementation ultimately must be solved at the level of the individual building where the actual persons are present who must develop teaching strategies, and this is true whether the curriculum is planned there or in some other arena. We shall return to this point again as is appropriate in the discussion of other components of curriculum engineering. It becomes crucial when we think of the involvement of people in curriculum planning and other operations in connection therewith. And the possibility has to be entertained that not all functions will go on in the same arena.

Selection and Involvement of People

A second group of theoretical issues lies in the selection and involvement of people in the various functions of curriculum engineering, namely, planning, implementation, and evaluation.

Historically at least, four different kinds of persons have been involved in curriculum decision-making but mostly in curriculum planning. They are: (1) specialized personnel, (2) representative groups composed of specialized personnel and some classroom teachers, (3) all professional personnel, and (4) all professional personnel plus representative lay citizens. Some would add pupils to this list, but it seems more likely that pupils should be involved at the level of instructional strategy rather than of curriculum decision-making.

Specialized personnel, in the meaning of the term as used here, refers to at least two groups of people. One consists of persons employed by school districts, or other agencies, specifically to do curriculum work, with the work in most cases, involving curriculum planning exclusively. These individuals customarily come from the ranks of teachers and supervisors, and they customarily are subject specialists, generalists, or trained curriculum specialists. What makes them specialized personnel is their involvement in curriculum decision-making activities. Schools and school districts have made use of such specialized personnel for many years. The second category, of more recent vintage, consists of persons who are specialized in a discipline and/or who have dominant interest in research in curriculum organization. These people have as their home bases universities or research centers. They rarely work on the total curriculum; instead they concentrate upon the development of a single discipline as part of a total curriculum. From time to time, school districts employ them as consultants to help with curriculum development, but they are not in-service curriculum workers in schools.

The involvement of specialized personnel and representative classroom teachers constitutes an extension of the use of specialized personnel. Such involvement assumes that the combination of specialized personnel and representative teacher groups will improve the effectiveness of curriculum decision-making. Presumably, it will be improved because of the recency of experience of the teachers in classrooms and because teachers will be able to exert leadership in implementation when the planning is completed. This level of involvement has been used most extensively in large city school systems; Chicago and Los Angeles are two examples. It capitalizes upon the expertness of specialized personnel; it takes advantage of the classroom teacher's point of view, and it is economically efficient in that only a small amount of released time is demanded.

The total involvement of professional personnel as a choice in curriculum engineering is more complicated than the first two. Total involvement means all classroom teachers, supervisors, special teachers, and administrators in a school or a school district. Advocates of this choice of involvement believe that the persons who make curriculum engineering decisions, who develop and execute instructional strategies, and who appraise the various school operations should participate in all three functions. In other words, if teachers and administrators are to participate in the systems of schooling that in this publication have been called the instructional system and the appraisal system, they should also participate in the curriculum system. In reality the only person who actually can participlate in all three systems is the teacher; administrators participate by exerting leadership to maintain and improve the systems. The theorist or practitioner who debates and decides on this involvement should know beforehand the teacher-load problems that it carries in its wake. The conventional impression of the job of the teacher is that his sole responsibility is to develop instructional strategies and carry them out with his class or classes. One realizes how strong this impression must be when one observes that teachers in elementary and secondary schools spend almost the entire day in a classroom with pupils trying to carry out pre-determined instructional strategies. The development of the strategies must come outside of the ordinary school day. To think of involving teachers additionally in anything as complicated as a curriculum system as it has been described in the preceding pages appears to be impossible. It is impossible unless ways and means for teachers to participate are found, and the principal ingredient in the ways and means is time unincumbered by teaching responsibility for work on curriculum tasks. Consequently, the two big questions about this choice of involvement are whether one believes that classroom teachers should be involved in curriculum engineering and whether one is willing to develop the ways and means for doing so assuming the answer to the first question is in the affirmative.

Cooperative lay-professional involvement is an extension of the involvement of all professional personnel inasmuch as the latter are included along with representative lay citizens who have concern about the schools. There is much controversy over the inclusion of lay-citizens in curriculum engineering, and many diverse interpretations about the proper role of citizens who are. Those opposed to the involvement claim that because curriculum-engineering processes are technical, they should be the sole prerogative of professional groups. Advocates of this position, in contrast, make much of the fundamental authority and responsibility of school patron groups, the extension of the partnership concept in public education, and the improved opportunities that it affords to educate more people in educational concerns. Most of the argument is at the level of value judgment for there is little research on the subject, certainly no comparative research.

It is impossible for anyone to think about the involvement of people in curriculum planning without relating it to the choice, or choices made, or needed to be made, in the arena for curriculum engineering. Any choice of people impinges on the curriculum-engineering arena, and vice versa. Let us take each of the possible arenas and examine the consequences for involvement.

In the case of the national arena, the only possible choice in involvement of people in curriculum planning is that of specialized personnel. It would be possible to include representative teachers, but if the country as a whole were to be represented, a very large group would have to be assembled. To think of total involvement of professional personnel would be ridiculous. However, planning is only one aspect of curriculum engineering. At the level of implementation, all classroom teachers employ the curriculum as a point of departure for their teaching. It would take almost monolithic control at the national level to engineer the implementation of a nationally planned curriculum in the national arena. The only reasonable alternative, in the case of those desiring to use the national arena for curriculum planning, is to split the curriculum engineering functions among two or more arenas. For example, it would be possible to use the national arena for curriculum planning and the individual school as the arena for implementation. We have only to look to France or Italy as illustrations of this type of split in curriculum engineering. In both of these countries, the arena for curriculum planning is the nation; curriculum planning is the responsibility of the national ministers of education. The responsibility for implementing the curriculum in both countries rests with the individual school. The link between the two arenas is the inspector who is the representative of the minister of education; it is his responsibility to insure that teachers do, in fact, implement the national curriculum.[1]

We have no similar situation in the United States. Yet individuals and groups at the national level and at regional levels do engage in curriculum activities of various kinds. For instance, scholars of national repute develop materials within their own disciplines. Contributors to curriculum outcomes also consist of scholarly groups such as the National Council for the Social Studies, the National Council of Teachers of English, the American Educational Research Association, the Association for Supervision and Curriculum Development, or the American Association for the Advancement of Sci-

[1]For a more complete analysis of this and other references that will be made to curriculum affairs in Europe, see George A. Beauchamp and Kathryn E. Beauchamp, *Comparative Analysis of Curriculum Systems* (Wilmette, Ill.: The Kagg Press, 1967).

ence. These too prepare and publish materials that are curricular in nature. But none prepares total curriculums to be used in schools; they are not part of a curriculum engineering system. They more appropriately fall into the category of individuals and groups who have influence upon the decisions of those formally involved in the functions of a curriculum engineering system. Their work products actually are input data for a curriculum system.

Because of the delegation of powers over education to school districts by the state governments in the United States, the state has not been extensively used as an arena for curriculum engineering. State departments of education frequently publish curriculum guides, but these generally are suggestive only rather than mandates for action in local school districts. In recent years, however, efforts have been made to strengthen the role of state departments of education in matters of leadership over affairs of schooling. The best illustration of these efforts is federal aid to education being administered through the state departments of education. It is not possible for anyone to predict at the moment whether the state actually will emerge as a functional arena for curriculum engineering. If it does, the same general pro and con statements applicable to the nation as an arena relatedly apply to the states. And the same problems of arena splitting and selection of personnel to be involved would maintain.

For all practical purposes, the involvement of personnel in large urgan school districts poses the same fundamental problems as it does in a state or the national arena. All professional personnel cannot be involved unless very drastic changes are made in present practices. As indicated before, the most frequently used arena for curriculum planning is the school district, and this applies to large urban centers as it does to small school districts. In the smaller school districts, however, it is possible to totally involve the professional personnel in curriculum planning, and it is also possible to additionally use representative lay citizens. Again, theorists and practitioners have the option of splitting the arena for curriculum engineering by assigning curriculum planning functions to the district arena and the implementation functions to the individual school. Whatever the choice of arena, or arenas, the full range of choices for involvement are available for consideration at the school district level.

The interesting thing about the individual school as the arena for curriculum engineering is that it immediately provides an arena in which all of the curriculum engineering functions may be performed readily. This is particularly true since involvement of teachers in curriculum planning may be followed immediately by involving the same persons in the tasks of curriculum implementation. The same persons also remain on the scene to participate in appraisal of the curriculum planning and implementation efforts. The "beauty" of the situation is that the individuals who develop the curriculum strategies are the same ones who develop and carry out the instructional strategies

An almost immediate reaction from people who seek uniformity among curriculum practices in either the district arena or a larger social-geographic arena is that equal opportunity is denied pupils in schools where curriculum efforts are not "as good" as in others. Caswell, a number of years ago,

> In brief, the "grass-roots" approach which views the individual school as the operational and planning unit does not mean that each school in a system should go its own way without regard for the others. It means, rather, that problems which are dealt with on a system-wide or partial-system basis should arise out of work done by individual school staffs and feed back into use through these staffs. The channel is from the individual school to the system and

back to the individual school rather than from the top down, as under the traditional system-wide approach.[2]

Caswell's statement leads us to propose the ensuing principle: No arena should be completely autonomous in making decisions about curriculum affairs. Illustratively, the individual school cannot be considered as having complete autonomy over its various functions; therefore, curriculum decisions made by higher authority for all schools under the jurisdiction of that authority must be accepted by the individual school unit. If a given state wishes to impose curriculum decisions on all schools and school districts within its borders, it may do so, and all are obliged to abide by those decisions. Nevertheless, the arena for incorporating all of these kinds of decisions into the functional curriculums of the schools remains with the individual school. A similar case could be made for the district as the arena choice. Similarly, the work of scholars in the disciplines and organized scholarly groups may be conceived as influences upon the decisions made in any arena, but the decisions are made only in the operational arena itself.

Organization and Procedures for Curriculum Planning

A third group of critical issues in curriculum theory is subsumed under the general heading of organizing and developing procedures for curriculum planning. In Figure 11, it was revealed that procedures are needed by those who determine curriculum goals, select a curriculum design, develop the details of the design, and actually do the writing of the curriculum. It is in this area that curriculum workers have had considerable experience here in the United States. Curriculums have been planned by the thousands, and many

[2]Hollis L. Caswell, *et. al., Curriculum Improvement in Public School Systems* (New York: Bureau of Publications, Teachers College, Columbia University, 1950), p. 78.

persons have been involved in the associated processes. Also many volumes have been written on the subject.

Organization of people to carry out curriculum planning procedures is dependent upon both the arena chosen for doing the curriculum planning and the kind and number of people involved in the planning activity. The problems and choices available to the theorist are not extensive when specialists are involved in curriculum planning, because these tend to be very few in number. Furthermore, they tend to work as a whole, devising their own unique ways of working together. Organization for curriculum planning becomes critical, however, when large and diversified numbers of people are involved. The complexities thus created constitute the theme of the following paragraphs.

One of the choices in organizing personnel to engage in curriculum planning was associated in the previous discussion with large urban centers or cities. This choice is a central office staff of curriculum specialists who have the principal responsibility for action and leadership in curriculum planning. To this group may be added representatives of the classroom teacher group, administrators, outside consultants, and/or representative lay citizens. The most common practice is for cities or large districts to organize the individuals involved into subject committees to prepare curriculum guides for the assigned subjects. Each committee tends to work independently, with the result that the total curriculum is an accumulation of separate subject pamphlets. A schedule for revision of the guides is usually established so that they are revised every three, four, or five years. Committees are disbanded when the planning task is completed, and new ones created at the time of the next revision. Havighurst reported on a system of this type for the city of Chicago.[3]

[3]Robert J. Havighurst, *The Public Schools of Chicago* (Chicago: The Board of Education of the City of Chicago, 1964), pp. 98-117.

In the small school district or the individual school arena, more possibilities for organizational schemes are apparent. In these arenas, it is feasible for curriculum engineers to involve all professional personnel and selected respresentative lay citizens if desired. The rule that must apply in this kind of circumstance is to create organization that will serve best the functions that have to be performed. It is common practice for curriculum planning groups to be headed by a curriculum council or a steering committee. Under such an arrangement, the council has the authority to organize groups and to reconstitute them as experience demands change.

The two major functions served by organization are to insure representation of all essential groups and to facilitate the tasks to be done. When the arena is the school district, all schools and all divisions in those schools may be represented on work committees or groups. Total involvement does not mean that all persons have to be involved in all specific tasks, but the organization must be such that all feel that they have been involved either through their own participation or through the participation of colleagues in whom they have faith to carry their share of the burden. No halo surrounds any particular organizing scheme because in tasks as complicated as those involved in curriculum planning no single scheme is consistently appropriate. Diverse curriculum groups and committees may be formed, including, for instance, study groups, discussion groups, consultant groups, leadership groups, subject committees, departmental committies, grade-level committees, system-wide committees, school committees, special committees, editing committees coordinating committees, and so forth. Such groups and committies are constituted, disbanded, or reconstituted depending upon need.

The most frequently used general procedures in curriculum planning are implied in the list of possible groups and committees cited in the previous paragraph. Group discussion is one. All curriculum planning endeavors will involve group discussion as an avenue to reaching curriculum decisions. Study is another. No planning groups should approach the task of writing a curriculum without having been exposed to the best recent thinking and research reflected in the contemporary curriculum literature. Curriculum planning should be an educative experience for those who participate in it, but it falls short of its potential if the participants do not engage in some form of study in the process. Use of consultants is a way of study; sometimes this is a very rewarding and efficient way of seeking new information. Writing is another important curriculum-making task. In any curriculum-planning venture there are many points at which ideas need to be recorded so that they may be reexamined and discussed. Obviously, the total curriculum needs to be written. These are the basic procedures that are fundamental to any scheme for curriculum planning.

Tasks to be completed constitute another aspect of curriculum planning procedures. In another writing, the author suggested a five-phase procedure for curriculum planning; it is illustrated in Figure 12.

The first phase of the suggested procedure is the formation of the curriculum council which acts as an overall coordinating agency. The second phase suggests that planning groups begin with an observance of present practices. In schools where no written curriculum has been in existence, it might be advantageous for them to make a written record of present practices. This recording affords individuals experience in writing curriculum materials at a familiar point. At the same time, it provides them with initial information for discussion and study. In schools where a curriculum has been in existence, but is thought to be obsolete, a careful study of the strengths and weaknesses of it would serve the same purpose.

Phase 1	Formation of the Curriculum Council
Phase 2	Appraisal of Contemporary Practices
Phase 3	Studying Curriculum Content
Phase 4	Formulation of Criteria
Phase 5	Constructing the Curriculum

Figure 12. *Suggested procedure phases for curriculum planning.* Adapted from George A. Beauchamp, *The Curriculum of the Elementary School* (Boston: Allyn and Bacon, Inc., 1964), p. 300.

Phase three embraces the study of new and alternative curriculum content. This period is the uplift, or most educative, aspect in the curriculum planning process for it is here that the planners acquire new knowledge. It is here they draw upon the numerous sources for creating a better curriculum. This phase may be thought of as actual inservice training of the participants in curriculum planning. Too often we expect teachers and others to do unfamiliar and complex tasks associated with curriculum planning when there is no real reason to expect that they have the competencies for doing them. In a carefully controlled study, Talmage[4] demonstrated that the more specific the training of personnel prior to their producing curriculum materials the better were the materials produced. Three treatments were used with the subjects: (1) inservice training on concept attainment, (2) conventional inservice training and (3) no training. Of these three treatments, the only one that made a significant difference in the ratings of the curriculum materials produced

[4]Harriet Talmage, *An Experimental Study in Curriculum Engineering* (Doctor's thesis, Northwestern University, Evanston, Illinois, 1967).

was the inservice training on concept attainment. This would also be the most appropriate time to make extended use of specialist consultants as part of the inservice education of the participants.

The fourth phase is to establish criteria for decisions about what shall go into the curriculum. Many decisions about what shall be included in a curriculum will be made on the basis of what is subjectively thought to be right or wrong, desirable or undesirable, good or bad. Because in most circumstances, there will be no scientific evidence to support choices, planning groups need a framework for making decisions in some consistent manner. The establishment of a set of criteria, or a set of "we believes," is one way of creating guidelines for those decisions. Among the categories of criteria that will be needed are criteria for goal selection, criteria for making decisions about curriculum design, and criteria for selecting and organizing subject matters as part of the design. Others may be added, and categories reclassified as required. But whatever categories are used, the process of creating the criteria will facilitate subsequent decision-making and will result in better curriculum consensus.

The final step of curriculum planning is the designing and writing of the curriculum. Included in it are such fundamental tasks as choosing a format for the instructional guide portion of the curriculum, examining various levels horizontally, checking total scope and sequence, and the actual processes of writing the document. Decisions have to be reached about what other sections shall be included in the curriculum other than the instructional guide section. It is during the designing and writing phase of curriculum engineering that much shifting of organizational groups will take place. It is important that articulation be provided for in the various school subjects from grade to grade, in fact throughout the entire twelve or thirteen years of schooling, but it is also important that concern be reflected in the planning processes for horizontal relationships among subjects or topics in terms of the total curriculum. For example, it is one thing to provide for the vertical articulation of a program in mathematics from kindergarten through grade twelve, or whatever the upper grade level of the school might be (vertical articulation), but it is quite a different matter to examine the totality of what a fifth-grade child is expected to be and become during a school year (horizontal articulation). Both of these problems require a shifting in organization of groups even though the same basic work procedures may be used.

The overall procedure described in the preceeding paragraph incorporates most of the activities proposed by curriculum authorities and used in projects reported by school systems. Variations reflect unique ways of working within the frameworks that groups have discovered to be effective for them. Most groups who undertake a curriculum planning project need to search for and to develop their own unique ways of working together to achieve their mutually accepted goals. Unquestionably, it is difficult for anyone to transplant specific procedures from persons and curriculum situations detached in time and place. Yet the basic tasks remain the same.

A reversal of this more or less commonly accepted procedure has been suggested by Taba. Taba suggested that instead of developing a general plan for the school program as an initial step it would be more profitable to start with the planning of teaching-learning units. In such a scheme, units would provide a basis for the general design.[5] The procedure seems to reverse the order of the two systems of schooling, curriculum and instruction. In other words, curriculum strategy would emerge from instructional strategy. This points up

[5]Hilda Taba, *Curriculum Development: Theory and Practice* (New York: Harcourt, Brace and World, Inc., 1962), pp. 441-442.

a very important theoretical problem. Which comes first? The important theoretical point is that the two positions provide a fundamental basis for the development of different curriculum theories.

Curriculum Implementation

Curriculum implementation means putting the curriculum to work. The two most justifiable reasons for a curriculum are as a point of departure for teaching and as a system for predicting behavioral outcomes. Curriculum implementation, in effect, consists of the processes necessary to accomplish these two purposes.

The first task in curriculum implementation is to arrange the school environment in such a way that the curriculum is used by teachers as a point of departure for their teaching. As indicated in Figure 10 at the beginning of this chapter, implementation takes place during the space-time representing the merger of the curriculum system with the instructional system. At this point, the curriculum becomes a working tool for teachers as they develop their instructional strategies. This is the point where the message of the curriculum planner is communicated to and interpreted by the teacher for a specific group, or for groups, of pupils. For a school to accomplish these ends, an agreed upon course of action needs to be determined and accepted by those who are to implement the curriculum. Assessment of changes in pupil behavior cannot be made until instruction takes place, but the planning of instructional strategy is an extension of the planned curriculum strategy. Both strategies seek behavioral outcomes which can only be brought to light subsequent to the teaching-learning activities.

Our history of curriculum implementation is weak. Many curriculums have been planned but much fewer have been systematically implemented. We are all familar with the circumstances in which the curriculum once it is produced collects dust on a shelf or is filed in the right-hand drawer of the teacher's desk. In the meantime, the teacher reverts to the same pattern of teaching that he used prior to the planning of the curriculum. Curriculum planning under these circumstances is a tremendous waste of human effort except for the concomitant educational gains for the planners.

A necessary prerequisite for curriculum implementation is the commitment by teachers to use the curriculum as a point of departure for the development of instructional strategies. The strength of the commitment may be enhanced by an implementation directive being part of the curriculum, teacher participation in the curriculum planning, and administrative leadership.

A suggested section of a curriculum is a clear statement of the use to be made of it. The statement may register the commitment and provide suggested procedures for implementing. We have had little experience with similar modes of recording in the United States, so specific illustrations are difficult to find. The schools of Italy, however, offer a very concrete illustration. In the new Italian middle school, a very systematic procedure is used. The curriculum for the middle schools is established by Parliament and the Minister of Public Instruction; all middle schools have the same curriculum. The curriculum is not an elaborate document, but it is clear as to what subjects are to be taught, the general range of each subject for each class, and the amount of time per week to be devoted to each subject. But along with the curriculum are instructions for implementation and adaptation. Each teacher is required to adapt the curriculum to his particular group of pupils, and furthermore, is required to demonstrate that he has done so. An elaborate system of forms and registers is provided for these purposes, and inspectors review these documents to determine if the curriculum has been followed and if the implementation procecedures have been executed.[6] The implementation procedures used in Italy would not mesh well with most practices in the United States, but they do illustrate how a planned curriculum may include provisions for implementation.

Curriculum implementation is facilitated if teachers who are to use the curriculum participate in its planning. Involvement, in effect, leads to follow through. This outcome was attested to by Johansen when he concluded that both individual teacher participation in curriculum planning activities and perception by teachers that they were influential in curriculum decision-making increased the likelihood of curriculum implementation.[7] Somewhat similar conclusions were reached by Heusner[8] and Nault,[9] but they cautioned against assuming that participation in curriculum planning alone would insure implementation. Other conditions are needed to support implementation efforts. Johansen would agree.

Since the principle of teacher involvement seems so self-evident, the question arises as to why teachers are not routinely required to participate in curriculum planning in most schools. The reasons offered by opponents of the principle generally carry considerable weight. One is that most teachers are not qualified to make curriculum decisions; that high caliber specialists in the various disciplines alone can do the

---

[6] See Beauchamp and Beauchamp, *op. cit.*, Chapter IV.

[7] Johansen, John H. *An Investigation of the Relationships between Teachers' Perceptions of Authoritative Influences in Local Curriculum Decision-Making and Curriculum Implementation* (Doctor's thesis, Northwestern University, Evanston, Illinois, 1965).

[8] Henry C. Heusner, *A Study of the Utilization of Curriculum* Guides as Related to Selection Factors in their Planning and Construction (Doctor's thesis, Wayne State University, Detroit, Michigan, 1963).

[9] William H. Nault, "Can Curriculum Guides be Effective?" *Educational Leadership*, 12:410-414, April, 1965.

job properly. Another is that teachers do not have time to devote to the time-consuming tasks of curriculum planning and development because their full work days are consumed with the execution of instructional strategies. A third is a combination of the first two; teachers should concentrate upon being good instructional strategists, and they should not be concerned with planning the curriculum. What is needed is carefully designed research to provide valid and reliable data, such as that cited previously by Johansen, leading to generalizations that will permit choices about involvement as it affects both the outcomes of planning and the processes of implementation.

Barriers to curriculum implementation are related to the degree to which teachers are committed to the curriculum that has been planned. The degree to which teachers feel the curriculum is appropriate for their students is an important barrier. Presumably, the curriculum is too rigid, it does not fit a particular group of pupils, or materials of instruction (textbooks in particular) are not available. One of the oldest fears of classroom teachers is that the curriculum will become fixed and rigid thereby seriously limiting their freedom of choice in classroom activity. Peculiarly enough, the same fear has not been associated with the adopted textbooks even thought they may be just as restrictive as any planned curriculum. The challenge here is for curriculum planners to create designs that are not rigid, and realistic implementation procedures.

Ability grouping practices in schools point to the question of need for separate curriculums for groups which differ on one or many dimensions. It was reported in the Havighurst survey of the Chicago public schools that many teachers claimed that the planned curriculum was not appropriate for pupils in their classes and schools![10] In this connection.

[10]*Op. cit.*

Larson did a carefully controlled study of acts of implementation by both inner-city and outer-city primary teachers in an urban school district wherein a commonly prescribed curriculum was used. Among the factors observed were the number of omissions and the number of additions made to the prescribed curriculum by teachers in both types of schools. Larson concluded that inner-city teachers tend to make more omissions than outer-city teachers, that outer-city teachers tend to make more additions than inner-city teachers, and that inner-city teachers tend to give less overall coverage to the curriculum than do outer-city teachers.[11] In attempts to solve this problem of pupil differences, a number of school systems are planning curriculums for two or three pupil groups: a normal group, an upper ability group, and a low ability disadvantaged group. Is the need for multiple curriculums lessened if the curriculum planning arena is the individual school? Is the need increased if a larger arena than the individual school is used for curriculum planning? What effect does involvement of teachers in curriculum planning have upon the problem? Little hard-nosed research is availble to provide answers to the above questions. At present they are being answered subjectively by those responsible for making curriculum decisions, nor do we fault this practice in most situations. A well-organized system for curriculum engineering, however, would make the answers more valid.

A consideration that is omitted too frequently from a discussion of the problems of curriculum implementation is the role of administrative personnel. The prognosis for successful implementation of a curriculum is weak when administrators are indifferent to its importance. Conversely, the prognosis is strong when administrators share with teachers

[11]Richard G. Larson, *The Implementation of an Urban School Curriculum by Inner-city and Outer-city Primary Teachers: A Comparative Study of Deviations from Prescribed Curricula* (Doctor's thesis, Northwestern University, Evanston, Illinois, 1968).

the importance of the curriculum being implemented systematically. Implementation is facilitated when administrative personnel accept the roles of chief engineers of the system.

Curriculum Evaluation

Although curriculum evaluation is rightfully a part of the total appraisal system of schooling, the execution of the evaluative aspects of curriculum functionally must be part of the curriculum system and therefore subject to curriculum engineering. There are at least four dimensions of curriculum evaluation; (1) evaluation of teacher use of the curriculum, (2) evaluation of the design, (3) evaluation of pupil outcomes, and (4) evaluation of the curriculum system. Experience with these four dimensions is very limited; therefore, most of what can be said about them has to be logically inferred.

Evaluation of teacher use is logically a first step in curriculum evaluation. The most simple data on teacher use are observations of the number of teachers who actually use the curriculum as a point of departure for their teaching. When teachers do not use the curriculum from which to develop their teaching strategies, curriculum evaluation stops at that point. Among the more plausible reasons for non-use are that teachers are unable or unwilling to develop supporting teaching strategies; teachers do not feel that they can or should depart from an adopted textbook; or they feel that the curriculum is not an adequate one. Conversely, evidence showing use of the curriculum as a point of departure by all teachers for developing teaching strategies constitutes convincing evidence about the dynamic quality of the curriculum. Quality of the use made is another matter. Possible indications of this consist of the number of additions, omissions, and adaptions effected to meet the differing needs of learners. Another consists of the kind of feedback for re-planning groups furnished by teachers because of their experiences with the curriculum. Another, but a very difficult one to measure in any sense, is the enthusiasm of teachers for participating in the curriculum system to the extent of making systematic use of the curriculum for developing instructional plans.

Evaluation of curriculum design is very difficult because of absence of criteria for doing so. Different designs are not available to be compared and matched against common criteria. To be sure, the success of teachers in use of a curriculum, as described in the previous paragraph, would have evaluative implications for the adequacy of the design. So would the success of the predictions made in the curriculum for pupil learning outcomes. Other criteria specifically related to design questions should direct the major aspects of the evaluation of curriculum design, but those criteria have yet to be formulated.

Of the four approaches to curriculum evaluation, assessment of the curriculum as an instrument to predict pupil outcomes is the most difficult to attain. The reason is that the entire instructional system of schooling intervenes (necessarily so, of course) between the time of curriculum planning and the observance of pupil learning. Many variables intervene.

Every aspect of the curriculum system must be brought under the microscope of evaluation, or the system deteriorates from lack of vitality. Feedback from the evaluation of the system must be available to rejuvenate the system's parts. The choice of arena, the choices made for involvement, organization of people for work, work procedures, and roles played by leadership personnel are all subjects to be appraised for strengths and weaknesses. These are the functions that make a curriculum system work. The feedback from evaluation of them helps to improve the system and to provide for continuity and growth from year to year.

A full range of techniques of measurement and appraisal is called for in curriculum evaluation. However, not all evidence produced by curriculum evaluation will be in quantitative form. Substantial evidence will be the subjective opinions of teachers which are vital in any scheme of curriculum evaluation. The number and kind of recommendations for change is useful information for making judgments about the system. Any change in the attitudes of people involved in curriculum engineering are indices of the effectiveness of the system. Our experience with curriculum evaluation is meager, and there is great need for curriculum workers to begin collecting all kinds of evidence to judge the worth of planned curriculums and curriculum systems.

SUMMARY

A curriculum system is a system for decision-making and action with respect to curriculum functions. A curriculum system has three primary functions: (1) to produce a curriculum, (2) to implement a curriculum, and (3) to appraise the effectiveness of a curriculum and a curriculum system. Curriculum engineering consists of all the processes and activities necessary to maintain and improve a curriculum system including leadership by such chief engineers as the superintendent, the principal, and the curriculum director.

In this chapter, the term schooling has been employed to cover those activities essential in the purposeful maintenance and operation of schools. Three of the more important systems of schooling were identified as the curriculum, the instructional, and the evaluation system. Our major concern is with the curriculum system. However, the interrelationships among the various systems serve to explain curriculum theory.

The language of systems analysis is applicable for describing a curriculum system. Input data for a curriculum system are derived primarily from educational foundations and past experience in curriculum affairs. The primary functions to be served by the content and processes of the system are to get a curriculum planned, to get it implemented through an instructional system, and to get it modified through evaluative feedback. The most tangible output of a curriculum system is a curriculum.

It is in the engineering of the various activities of the curriculum system that the most apparent theoretical issues emerge. The choice of arena for curriculum engineering from the nation, the state, the district, or the school is fundamental. Curriculum engineering can function in any one or in any combination of these arenas.

Exactly who is to be involved in curriculum decision-making constitutes an important consideration of curriculum engineering. The most obvious choices are specialized personnel, representative specialists and teachers, all professional personnel, and all professional personnel plus representative lay citizens. There is very close relationship between choice of arena and choice of people to be involved.

Two basic considerations dictate organization and procedures for curriculum planning. One is the size of the group to be involved in the planning, and the other is the number of tasks or steps that are to be undertaken. The complexity of organization increases as groups become larger. Curriculum planning by large groups is too complex to strive for permanent task groups with the possible exception of the curriculum council or the steering committee. Procedures tend to dictate organization, and in turn, tasks tend to dictate many procedures.

Curriculum implementation consists of the processes necessary to get the curriculum used as a point of departure for developing teaching strategies. Regardless of choices made concerning arena or involvement for planning, the classroom teacher is the only person who can do the implementing. Consequently, teacher commitment to do so is fundamental to success in implementation. In this connection, teacher participation in curriculum planning is one of the most successful devices for eliciting the commitment. Barriers to implementation include lack of commitment, feelings by teachers that a curriculum is inappropriate for pupils, and lack of leadership by administrative personnel.

Curriculum evaluation involves evaluating teacher use of of the curriculum, the design, pupil outcome predictions, and the curriculum system. Limited experience in this area points up the drastic need for case studies and research that will lead to suggested procedures and theoretical generalizations.

SUGGESTED READINGS

American Educational Research Association. "Curriculum Planning and Development," *Review of Educational Research*, 27:237-304, June, 1957

American Educational Research Association. "Curriculum Planning and Development," *Review of Educational Research*, 30:181-279, June, 1960.

American Educational Research Association. "Curriculum Planning and Development," *Review of Educational Research*, 33:227-337, June, 1963.

American Educational Research Association. "Curriculum Planning and Development," *Review of Educational Research*, 36:339-389, June, 1966.

Ammons, Margaret and Robert S. Gilchrist. *Assessing and Using Curriculum Content.* Washington, D. C.: the Association for Supervision and Curriculum Development, NEA, 1965.

Anderson, Dan W., James B. Macdonald, and Frank B. May (eds.). *Strategies of Curriculum Development.* Columbus: Charles E. Merrill Books, Inc., 1965.

Anderson, Vernon, E. *Principles and Procedures of Curriculum Development.* Second edition. New York: The Ronald Press Company, 1965.

Association for Supervision and Curriculum Development, NEA. *Curriculum Change: Direction and Process.* Washington, D. C.: the Association, 1966.

Association for Supervision and Curriculum Development, NEA. *Research for Curriculum Improvement.* Yearbook 1957, Washington, D. C.: the Association, 1957.

Association for Supervision and Curriculum Development, NEA. *What Are the Sources of the Curriculum? A Symposium.* Washington, D. C.: the Association, 1962.

Beauchamp. George A. *The Curriculum of the Elementary School.* Boston: Allyn and Bacon, Inc., 1964.

Beauchamp, George A. and Kathryn E. Beauchamp. *Comparative Analysis of Curriculum Systems.* Wilmette, Ill.: The Kagg Press, 1967.

Broudy, Harry S., B. Othanel Smith, and Joe R. Burnett. *Democracy and Excellence in American Secondary Education.* Chicago: Rand McNally and Company, 1964.

Cay, Donald F. *Curriculum: Design for Learning.* New York: The Bobbs-Merrill Company, Inc., 1966.

Conner, Forrest E. and William J. Ellena (eds.) *Curriculum Handbook for School Administrators.* Washington, D. C.: American Association of School Administrators, NEA, 1967.

Doll, Ronald C. *Curriculum Improvement: Decision-Making and Process.* Boston: Allyn and Bacon, Inc., 1964.

Faunce, Roland C. and Nelson L. Bossing. *Developing the Core Curriculum.* Second edition. Englewood Cliffs, N. J.: Prentice-Hall, Inc., 1958.

Gwynn, J. Minor. *Curriculum Principles and Social Trends.* Third edition. New York: The Macmillan Company, 1960.

Inlow, Gail M. *The Emergent in Curriculum.* New York: John Wiley and Sons, Inc., 1966.

Johansen, John H. "The Relationships between Teachers' Perceptions of Influence in Local Curriculum Decision-making and Curriculum Implementation," *The Journal of Educational Research*, 61: 81-83. October, 1967.

King, Arthur R. and John A. Brownell. *The Curriculum and the Disciplines of Knowledge.* New York: John Wiley and Sons, 1966.

Krug, Edward A. *Curriculum Planning.* Revised edition. New York: Harper and Row, Inc., 1957.

Leese, Joseph, Kenneth Frasure, and Mauritz Johnson, Jr. *The Teacher in Curriculum Making.* New York: Harper and Row, Inc., 1961.

McNally, Harold J., A. Harry Passow, and Associates. *Improving the Quality of Public School Programs.* New York: Bureau of Publications, Teachers College, Columbia University, 1960.

Neagley, Ross L. and N. Dean Evans. *Handbook for Effective Curriculum Development.* Englewood Cliffs, N. Y.: Prentice-Hall, Inc., 1967.

Oliver, Albert I. *Curriculum Improvement.* New York: Dodd, Mead and Company, 1965.

Passow, A. Harry (ed.). *Curriculum Crossroads.* New York: Bureau of Publications, Teachers College, Columbia University, 1962.

Project on the Instructional Program of the Public Schools, NEA. *Deciding What to Teach.* Washington, D. C., the Project, 1963.

Project on the Instructional Program of the Public Schools, NEA. *Planning and Organizing for Teaching.* Washington, D. C., the Project, 1963.

Ragan, William B. *Modern Elementary Curriculum.* Third edition. New York: Holt, Rinehart and Winston, Inc., 1966.

Saylor, J. Galen and William M. Alexander. *Curriculum Planning for Modern Schools.* New York: Holt, Rinehart and Winston, Inc., 1966.

Smith B. Othanel, William O. Stanley, and J. Harlan Shores. *Fundamentals of Curriculum Development.* Revised edition. Yonkers-on-Hudson: World Book Company, 1957.

Sowards, G. Wesley and Mary-Margaret Scobey. *The Changing Curriculum and the Elementary Teacher.* San Francisco: Wadsworth Publishing Company, Inc., 1961.

Stratemeyer, Florence and others. *Developing A Curriculum for Modern Living.* Revised edition. New York: Bureau of Publications, Teachers College, Columbia University, 1957.

Taba, Hilda. *Curriculum Development: Theory and Practice.* New York: Harcourt, Brace, and World, Inc., 1962.

Tyler Ralph W. *Basic Principles of Curriculum and Instruction.* Chicago: University of Chicago Press, 1950.

Wiles, Kimball. *The Changing Curriculum of the American High School.* Englewood Cliffs, N. J.: Prentice-Hall, Inc., 1963.

7

CURRICULUM AS

A FIELD OF STUDY

Curriculum as a field of study is a third way the term "curriculum" is used. It is one customarily engaged in by graduate students and instructional personnel at colleges and universities. Participants in in-service curriculum programs during the time of their involvement belong in this category. The areas for their study include curriculum engineering, curriculum design, curriculum theory, and the foundational sources for them.

As we have stated or implied a number of times previously, the field of curriculum is a morass of undefined concepts used without careful definition by many. And when basic concepts are not selected and defined carefully, the boundaries between curriculum and other components of education become blurred. This is true particularly with respect to the boundaries and relationships among curriculum, instruction, evaluation, and learning. Distinctions made in earlier chapters emphasized the need for identifying unique properties and functions. There are many, however, who reject the idea that distinctions should be made among curriculum, instruction, evaluation, and learning. There also are differences in opinion about the domain of a curriculum. We refer here to the use of a single subject, or a discipline, as "curriculum" versus the use of "curriculum" as a referent to the entire program of a school.

In this kind of situation, the theoretical issues in the field can best be noted by an analysis of the conditions and circumstances within the field as revealed in curriculum literature.

CURRICULUM TEXBOOKS AND COURSES

One way of appraising the field of curriculum is to examine treatments of the field given in textbooks devoted to the subject. There are several different kinds of textbooks written on curriculum. One type is a wide-coverage book dealing primarily with curriculum development but including chapters on curriculum foundations and curriculum design. A significant portion of this type of book is devoted to the topics treated in the previous chapter on curriculum engineering.

Another type is the curriculum book that discusses the content and organization of school subjects. These may also have one or more chapters devoted to curriculum planning.

A third type is one in which topics are treated as though curriculum and instruction should be treated as a common domain. These customarily contain discussions of content, materials of instruction, and modes of teaching for each of the school subjects. Textbooks such as these often contain discussions of administrative organization including non-gradedness, tracking, team teaching, and a brief discussion of planning.

Many curriculum books vary from these types by combining elements of each and by diverse treatments of fundamental curriculum concepts. Books of readings in curriculum contain the greatest mixtures of all.

When publishers produce textbooks on curriculum, they do so in the belief that they will be used in college and university courses, and they generally are. The implication here is that courses must vary as much in purpose and content as the textbooks do. Range and variation in curriculum course offerings is another indication of the confusion that reigns in the field of curriculum.

The condition of course offerings in curriculum is typified by a study by Bateman.[1] He surveyed the course offerings in elementary currciulum offered by universities having undergraduate programs in elementary teacher education. The results of the study dramatically pointed out that content variation is a characteristic of such courses. When applying to elementary teacher education, the courses tend to cover the whole gamut of elementary education.

Wootton also surveyed curriculum offerings in teacher education institutions.[2] He reported many observations similar to those of Bateman. Wootton, however, was more convinced than Bateman that the language of curriculum is being refined.

Most courses devoted to curriculum planning are taught at the graduate level. In this connection. Altman analyzed the

[1]Donald G. Bateman, *An Investigation of the Circumstances and Conditions of the Undergraduate Course in Elementary School Curriculum in Teacher Education Programs in Selected Universities in the United States* (Doctor's thesis, Northwestern University, Evanston, Illinois, 1966).

[2]Lutian R. Wootton, "The Curriculum: Is the Concept Changing?" *Clearing House*, 42:143-145, 1967.

positions taken by authors on curriculum planning[3] He developed a model for classifying treatments of objectives in curriculum planning and the activities recommended for achieving those objectives. Altman found great differences in both objectives and activities for curriculum planning in the various positions. Content variation in curriculum planning books is an indication that similar variation takes place in courses devoted to curriculum development.

RESEARCH

The journal most concerned with reviewing research in education is the *Review of Educational Research.* Every three years the June issue of the journal has curriculum as its central theme. A substantial number of the contributors to the issues devoted to curriculum have noted the paucity of curriculum research.

An interesting picture of the status of curriculum research is revealed in the 1960, the 1963, and the 1966 June issues of the *Review.* The three issues contain twenty-one chapters. Three of the twenty-one contain discussions of the state of the field. Four fall under the general heading of forces influencing curriculum decisions. Two are devoted to curriculum components or design. Two chapters highlight teaching. Three review curriculum development processes. The conditions of curriculum theory and research are the topics of four. And three of the twenty-one chapters are devoted to materials and media. One of the three issues contains five chapters, another ten chapters, and the third six chapters, but

---

[3]Burton E. Altman, *An Identification and Classification of Selected Characteristics of Cooperative Curriculum Planning Positions from 1918 to 1965* (Doctor's thesis, Northwestern University, Evanston, Illinois, 1965).

this does not mean that topics treated in the ten-chapter issue were not treated more briefly somewhere in the other two. Many were. Nevertheless, this analysis of chapters gives some picture of the concerns of persons interested in curriculum research.

More specifically, Goodlad concluded in 1960 that: "Curriculum theorizing to date is best described as abstract speculation; curriculum research as 'dust-bowl' empiricism; and curriculum practice as rule-of-thumb guesswork . . . ."[4] To this Abramson added the following in 1966:

> The curriculum field has been very rich in statements of philosophy and principles but, . . . is lacking in theoretical formulations which engender researchable hypotheses. Because of both the attempt to conduct research on the basis of the holistic view of curriculum and the derivative nature of its methodology, curriculum research has been based predominantly on pupil testing, as has research in teaching and instruction.[5]

Abramson raises here the question of criteria for evaluation of curriculums and curriculum practices. Macdonald challenged the use of pupil learning as a criterion for curriculum evaluation. He suggested that once a curriculum is the output of a curriculum system, it would be more appropriate to use such criteria as degree of use of the curriculum made by teachers, teacher attitudes toward the curriculum, and so forth.[6]

It is apparent from reviews of research on curriculum that the research effort has not been making major contributions to the definition of curriculum as a field. The basic problems of scientific theorizing in curriculum have not been faced, or resolved, by curriculum researchers, too few of whom are

[4]John I. Goodlad, "Curriculum: The State of the Field," *Review of Educational Research*, 30:195, June, 1960.

[5]David A. Abramson, "Curriculum Research and Evaluation," *Review of Educational Research*, 36:389, June, 1966.

[6]James B. Macdonald, "Curriculum Theory: Problems and A Prospectus" (a mimeographed paper presented at the meeting of Professors of Curriculum, Miami Beach, 1964).

specialists in curriculum theory.

COMMON AND UNCOMMON DENOMINATORS

Authors in the field of curriculum write about a wide variety of topics and with considerable variation in use of fundamental concepts. Problems in communication and research arise from such divergent topics and concept variation. Nonetheless, a cluster of relevant topics prevades much of the curriculum literature. Curriculum theorists need to identify and characterize both the common and uncommon denominator of curriculum as a field of study. Such activity by theorists should lead to more sophisticated and to more sharply differentiated curriculum theories.

Foundational Influences

Most authors of textbooks on curriculum include chapters on such subjects as history of curriculum efforts, principles or theories of learning, human growth and development, cultural and social information about schools including political forces, and philosophy of education. These subjects have been treated as the foundations of education in general, with scholars in each specific component of education, including curriculum, drawing from them information and authority for much of their work. The significance of foundational influences upon education is highlighted by positions occupied by people in professional education. Each foundational area has a parent in the disciplines — educational psychology has one in psychology, philosophy of education in philosophy, educational sociology in sociology, and so forth. But education is an applied discipline, and it is the job of the educational psychologist, the philosopher of education, and the sociologist to apply knowledge from their parent disciplines to education. The same is true for students of the field of curriculum. They must study the import of knowledge from related disciplines for the characteristics and functions of curriculum.

There are three ways in which the student of curriculum should be concerned with foundations. First, as a designer of subject matter, the curriculum worker needs to know the rationales for organizing school subjects as prerequisite information for selecting and organizing materials for a school's curriculum. The sources for most of those rationales lie in the parent disciplines. Second, the student of curriculum needs to know about past experiences in school affairs with curriculum. There is no justification for his acting from ignorance when he can avoid it. Third, and very important, the curriculum student and worker must have insight into human behavior including the value component in individual and group behavior. The curriculum planner must anticipate pupil learning, and to do so he must have information that will justify such predictions. The leader in curriculum work needs to have human engineering understandings inasmuch as his greatest trials come in organizing and manipulating human beings in curriculum work in schools.

Foundational data are input data to any curriculum system. The curriculum worker selects and uses data in anticipation of the functions to be performed within the curriculum system. The curriculum theorist must explain the probable consequences for whatever selections are made in terms of other choices that have to be made in curriculum design or curriculum engineering. Few students of curriculum would deny the necessity for including the continuing study of foundations as part of the field of curriculum inasmuch as these exert so many influences upon what may and should be done in curriculum.

Other Curriculum Components

There is no need for us to review the previous discussions about other curriculum components here. Few, if any, would deny that the problems and issues of curriculum design and organization of specific school subjects belong in the domain of curriculum. Conversely, many would disagree about specific dimensions of those problems and issues.

Similarly, curriculum engineering is an established component of curriculum. A curriculum must be planned if it is to exist. Once in existence, people need to implement it. Avowedly, it should be revised continuously. The latter demands evaluation. Diverse practices reflect different curriculum positions, but they nevertheless belong in the field of curriculum.

Most agree that research and theory building are components of the field of curriculum. There is a paucity of both, but substantial progress in curriculum as a field of study is dependent upon them. All of the aforementioned areas of agreement and disagreement are primary sources for research ideas and for theory building efforts.

SUMMARY

Two generalizations emerge from the discussion presented in this chapter. First, there is substantial agreement that certain large areas belong in the domain of curriculum as a field of study. The most frequently discussed areas are curriculum foundations, school subjects, design, curriculum engineering, research, and theory development. Second, writers show considerable disparity in meanings associated with fundamental concepts in curriculum. Chief among these are definitions of a curriculum, conceived uses for a curriculum, and the processes of curriculum development.

The work of curriculum theorists is an encouraging phenomenon. Theorists have the opportunity to capitalize upon the common and uncommon denominators of the present status of the curriculum field by using them as springboards for better theories and for more unique theories. In the process, curriculum as a field of study should become more clarified.

SUGGESTED READINGS

Note: Most of the suggested readings at the end of Chapter 7 also are relevant here.

Altman, Burton E. *An Identification and Classification of Selected Characteristics of Cooperative Curriculum Planning Positions from 1918 to 1965.* Doctor's thesis. Northwestern University, Evanston, Illinois, 1965.

Association for Supervision and Curriculum Development, NEA. *Research for Curriculum Improvement.* 1957 Yearbook. Washington, D. C.: the Association, 1957.

Bateman, Donald G. *An Investigation of the Circumstances and Conditions of the Undergraduate Course in Elementary School Curriculum in Teacher Education Programs in Selected Universities in the United States.* Doctor's thesis. Northwestern University, Evanston, Illinois, 1966.

Huebner, Dwayne (ed.). *A Reassessment of the Curriculum.* New York: Bureau of Publications, Teachers College, Columbia University, 1964.

Kerr, J. F. *The Problem of Curriculum Reform.* Leicester, England: Leicester University Press, 1967.

Leeper, Robert R. (ed.). *Assessing and Using Curriculum Content.* Washington, D. C.: Association for Supervision and Curriculum Development, 1965.

Leeper, Robert R. (ed.). *Curriculum Change: Direction and Process.* Washington, D. C.: Association for Supervision and Curriculum Development, 1966.

Leeper, Robert R. (ed.). *What Are the Sources of the Curriculum? A Symposium.* Washington, D. C.: Association for Supervision and Curriculum Development, 1962.

Macdonald, James B. and Robert R. Leeper (eds.). *Language and Meaning.* Washington, D. C.: Association for Supervision and Curriculum Development, 1966.

Parker, J. Cecil and Louis J. Rubin. *Process as Content: Curriculum Design and the Application of Knowledge.* Chicago: Rand McNally and Company, 1966.

Robinson, Helen R. (ed.). *Precedents and Promise in the Curriculum Field.* New York: Teachers College Press, Teachers College, Columbus University, 1966.

Smith, B. Othanel and Robert H. Ennis. *Language and Concepts in Education.* Chicago: Rand McNally and Company, 1961.

Venable, Tom C. *Philosophical Foundations of the Curriculum.* Chicago: Rand McNally and Company, 1967.

Wootton, Lutian R. "The Curriculum: Is the Concept Changing?" *Clearing House,* 42:143-145, November, 1967.

8

VALUES IN

CURRICULUM THEORY

Values are products of our culture, generated by both individuals and groups. For us to say that values are important driving forces in the maintenance of the human condition is an understatement. And for an important social institution like the school not to transmit and generate values is incredible. Individuals acquire certain values by a general process of enculturation; they acquire others didactically. The process of schooling employs both approaches.

If it is assumed that formal education needs to be concerned with the teaching of values, values become a curriculum problem. In this connection, curriculum planners have generally tended to avoid the issues involved, and curriculum theorists have done little better. The demand for curriculum attention to values is evidenced by Smith, Stanley, and Shores in the following:

> The heart of a culture is its universals. The heart of the
> universals is the values or, in other words, the rules by
> which people order their social existence. These rules, when
> built into the personalities of the individuals comprising the
> society, create the personality type peculiar to the culture.
> Hence, the heart of any satisfactory educational program
> consists of those basic values that give meaning to the
> purposes, plans, and activities of the individual.[1]

As indicated in a different context in Chapter 5, within
the realm of curriculum theory, value considerations are
primarily a problem of curriculum design. Our purpose in this
chapter is to develop the rationale for value considerations
rather than to identify and elaborate the specifics of design.
First, we take a brief look at some of the ramifications of
value interpretations as they generally are presented; we then
follow with implications for curriculum theory.

VALUE INTERPRETATIONS

Values, in essence, are the rules by which people shape
their behavior. They generally are multi-dimensional. They
reflect attitudes or dispositions of individuals to feel and act
in given ways. Values embody such concepts as good or bad,
homely or pretty, rude or polite, unacceptable or acceptable.
Values also involve criteria by which people form dispositions. Kaplan designated a two-way classification when
he said, "Values may be distinguished as *instrumental* or
inherent according to whether they are prized in themselves

---

[1]B. Othanel Smith, William O. Stanley, and J. Harlan Shores, *Fundamentals
of Curriculum Development* (revised edition; Yonkers-on-Hudson: World Book
Company, 1957), p. 85.

or because they are believed to lead to something else which we prize." [2]

The Domain of Values

Philosophers with differing outlooks or original assumptions tend to interpret values differently. Both Hardie[3] and Park[4] place value theorists in three groups: the intuitive, the skeptical, and the pragmatic. Park summarized the three positions as follows:

> The intuitive theory emphasizes the "ultimate" nature of values and man's supposed ability to recognize the ultimate. The skeptic places his emphasis upon the impossibility of moving from beliefs to imperatives. The pragmatist is interested in the existential context in which valuations are made and insists upon determining what is good or bad by probable or actual consequences of acting in terms of a particular judgment.[5]

Whatever the position may be, the general purpose of having a value theory is to provide "a set of guide lines for the meaning and ground of value judgments."[6] Later in the chapter we discuss the implications of value theories for the curriculum theorist; however, the significance of that discussion we feel, will be enhanced by looking first into the kinds of questions and problems raised in the area of values.

There seem to be at least two aspects of most value ques-

[2]Abraham Kaplan, *The Conduct of Inquiry* (San Francisco: Chandler Publishing Company, 1964), p. 393.

[3]C. D. Hardie, "The Idea of Value and the Theory of Education," *Educational Theory*, 7:196-199, July, 1957.

[4]Joe Park, "Values and Education," *Education in Urban Society*, edited by B. J. Chandler, Lindley J. Stiles and John I. Kitsuse (New York: Dodd Mead and Company, Inc., 1962), pp. 233-248.

[5]*Ibid.*, p. 242.

[6]Kaplan, *op. cit.*, p. 387.

tions. One has to do with the rules for behavior per se; the other, with behavioral adaptations to the rules. These two dimensions are expressed in different ways. For example, Frankena distinguished between Moral Education X (MEX) and Moral Education Y (MEY). MEX was used to designate the handing on (through education) knowledge of good and evil or knowing how to act. MEY referred to education to ensure that individual and group conduct will conform with the knowledge of MEX.[7] Axtelle distinguished between psychological values (matters of fact) and axiological values (what we ought to value).[8] He noted the difference between "the enjoyed and the enjoyable, the desired and the desirable, the satisfying and the satisfactory."[9] Raths, Harmin, and Simon represented such value phenomena as goals, attitudes, feelings, beliefs, interests, and others as value indicators. They termed choosing, prizing, and acting as the processes of valuing.[10] Broudy, Smith, and Burnett proposed that value education has two principal outcomes. One of them is appreciation. The other is the development of strategies for making choices.[11] Whatever the language used may be, there persist two sides of the value question — the rules themselves and the processes of human recognition and acceptance of those rules as governors of behavior.

[7]William K. Frankena, "Toward a Philosophy of Moral Education," *Harvard Educational Review*, 28:300-313, Fall, 1958.

[8]George E. Axtelle, "The Humanizing of Knowledge and the Education of Values," *Educational Theory*, 16:101-109, April, 1966.

[9]*Ibid.*, p. 107.

[10]Louis E. Raths, Merrill Harmin, and Sidney B. Simon, *Values and Teaching* (Columbus: Charles E. Merrill Books, Inc., 1966), pp. 30-33.

[11]Harry S. Broudy, B. Othanel Smith, and Joe R. Burnett, *Democracy and Excellence in American Secondary Education* (Chicago: Rand McNally and Company, 1964), p. 219.

The Humanistic and the Scientific

One gets the general impression from at least certain contemporary literature that the humanistic domain is value-centered whereas the scientific domain is fact-centered. In the bibliography at the end of this chapter, for example, literature is cited bearing such titles as *Humanizing Education, The Humanities and the Curriculum,* and *Science and the Humanities.* Basically, the distinctions between humanistic studies and scientific studies have to do with human use and goals. Prior expressed a difference between the final products of scientific activity and humanistic activity as follows:

> . . . the final product of scientific activity is impersonal and uncommitted in any way to any particular human use or goal; the final product of literary effort, on the other hand, is inevitably identified with its author's character and his personal artistry, and it cannot escape its involvement with particular human feelings and with a particular view of human conduct and human aspirations and goals.[12]

Many would take objection to Prior's statement based on grounds that the product may be value-free but the scientist himself is not. Kaplan, for example, points out that it is dubious whether the scientist actually is concerned only with an impersonal search for truth. He notes that the preponderance of applied research stems from needs for solutions to practical problems.[13] No doubt the argument about the value-free status of the scientist will go on for years to come, but the controversy helps to keep man more conscious of the import of values for his behavior.

In this connection, facts and values are not necessarily mutually exclusive. Many value statements are supportable

[12]Moody E. Prior, *Science and the Humanities* (Evanston, Ill.: Northwestern University Press, 1962), p. 17.

[13]*Op. cit.,* p. 389.

by factual evidence. In a discussion of scientific determina-
tion of value judgments, Hook stated:

> A scientific or rational approach to judgments of value
> consists in (a) the investigation of the causes of such
> judgments, (b) their logical implications, and (c) their
> probable consequences. This investigation is always to be
> undertaken in relation to alternative values which limit
> freedom of choice.[14]

The converse is true too. Values become criteria for courses
of action leading to empirical information. A teacher who
has high regard for rote memoritor learning judges his pupils
on evidence from their rote and memoritor performances.
Comparably, a teacher who places high premium on the more
heuristic techniques in learning judges his pupils on evidence
of ability to make observations, to collect information, to use
resources, to reach rational generalizations, and so forth.
Values so used become principles for guiding action. They
first are learned; then they become tools for teaching or for
learning.

VALUES AND THE CURRICULUM

Any discussion of values as related to the curriculum
of a school needs to begin with educational aims. Most
educational aims are stated as if schools ought to accomplish
designated ends. The aims thus are statements of value judgment. For example, we may state that an aim of the secondary school is to improve citizenship. In value terms, we
would be stating that the school ought to do something to
improve the citizenship behavior of its pupils. Note that the

---

[14]Sidney Hook, *Education for Modern Man* (new edition; Alfred A. Knopf,
1963), p. 179.

statement includes no attempt to describe citizenship behavior, and therefore, it gives no direction for the teaching of citizenship behaviors nor for the measuring of the effects of teaching. In this circumstance, it is apparent that the generalized aim needs to be translated into the language of curriculum strategy and instructional strategy. The translation of aims into curriculum strategy and instructional strategy becomes the means of the end-means continuum.

It is in the realm of aim declaration that much of our modern controversy lies with respect to values. One may state that an aim of schooling is to teach the young to be literate, that is, to teach them to read and write their language. This aim is only value laden at the point of deciding that this function should be carried out by schools rather than by some other agency of society. Conversely, for one to state that an aim of schooling is to foster an ideal of a common human community or to develop a rugged individualistic and nationalistic spirit is heavily value laden. Educational planners have had success in developing curricular and instructional strategies as means for achieving the ends of the literacy aim, but they have done virtually nothing with the latter.

As we indicated earlier, some values are acquired by the young through the processes of general enculturation. Others have to be taught. Very frequently, the values acquired through general enculturation are in conflict with those selected to be taught in schools. Some very vivid examples are occurring in our communities today, and not all of them in large urban communities. One of these is the values implied by the open hostility of certain ethnic and/or religious groups toward Negroes and other minority groups. Yet most of the persons who exhibit such hostility would profess that they believe in the equality of man and in equality of opportunity for all mankind, and on Sunday mornings in churches, they routinely avow to believe in the brotherhood of man. The purpose here is to illustrate that many attempts on the part of schools to affect significantly the value of orientations of their pupils may run counter to the forces of enculturation.

Selecting Curriculum Content

Most of the foregoing discussion in this chapter leads to the conclusion that schools cannot escape acceptance of responsibility for the transmission of values. It goes without saying that the transmission of values would include values conceived both as knowledge of rules of behavior, and as a set of processes leading to personal acceptance of the rules of behavior. Now, we turn to what may be included in curriculums so that the transmission can take place at the level of instruction.

The first task for curriculum planners with respect to values is to identify and state those expressed as attitudes, beliefs, ideals, or concepts that the school should bring to the attention of pupils. O'Connor suggested that these should consist of "a set of values or ideals embodied and expressed in the purposes for which knowledge, skills and attitudes are imparted . . . . " [15] Broudy, Smith and Burnett stated:"Three kinds of norms should be taken into account as the content of the curriculum is selected. These are the norms of efficiency or prescriptive rules, regulatory norms, and moral norms."[16]

The values of any society are embedded in its culture. Smith, Stanley, and Shores identified three elements in which the core of the American value system lies — the democratic

[15]*Op. cit.,* p. 5.

[16]*Op. cit.,* p. 150.

tradition, the belief in the maximum development of the individual, and the institutions established to perpetuate the values.[17] In a somewhat similar vein, Inlow cited three origins of our time-tested values: "(1) in the conditions of practical living throughout the ages, (2) in man's progressive and culumative assessment of these conditions, and (3) in a progressively growing body of theoretical dogma . . . ."[18] But these are very general terms. The decision-making for the curriculum planner is much more complicated.

Something that is often overlooked in curriculum work is that the very choice of subjects for a school is a value choice. It is assumed, for example, that the choice of seven, eight, or nine subjects for elementary schools will provide the general-education type program believed to be essential for children of elementary-school age. It is also loosely assumed that the use of those subjects as the organizational framework for the educational program will fulfill the overall aims of education for children in the society.

Unquestionably, statements of aims do not lead directly to the selection of school subjects as means for attaining those aims. The aims, by definition, imply that schools should be instrumental in achieving certain ends. There ought to be a criteria relationship between the aims and the subjects selected to advance them, but there too seldom is. Both curriculum theorists and curriculum planners need to examine this problem more critically.

Within most, if not all, school subjects, there are value components. Phenix[19] classified the realms of meaning as symbolics, empirics, esthetics, synnoetics, ethics, and syn-

[17]*Op. cit.*, pp. 76-82.

[18]Gail M. Inlow, *The Emergent in Curriculum* (New York: John Wiley and Sons, Inc., 1966), pp. 5-6.

[19]Philip H. Phenix, *Realms of Meaning* (New York: McGraw-Hill Book Company, 1964).

optics. Some, if not all, of these realms are value sources. The humanities and the social studies are considered to be important sources for values. All of the disciplines have unique groups of value concepts. All have their own modes of behaving and classes of problem. Nevertheless, there is a great deal of difference in the value load of subjects like music or literature and mathematics or physics.

Stating Behavioral Objectives

In much curriculum literature, a distinction is made between the general aims of education and the specific behavioral objectives to be fostered by the systems of schooling. Using the general aims as a basis, a major task for the curriculum planner is the stating, classifying, and arranging within the curriculum of the behavioral objectives. It is commonplace for us to say that behavioral objectives fall into three categories: the cognitive, the psycho-motor, and the affective. The three actually are applicable to any subject, but they have different weightings from subject to subject. Our concern at the moment is mostly with the affective domain. In this connection, some guidelines for the curriculum planner are available even though they come from a single source. The publication, *A Taxonomy of Educational Objectives, Handbook II: Affective Domain* classifies value objectives into five categories in ascending complexity. The following is a condensation of the taxonomical structure for affective behaviors listed in that publication:

    1.0   Receiving (attending)
        1.1 Awareness
        1.2 Willingness to receive
        1.3 Controlled or selected attention

2.0 Responding
    2.1 Acquiescence in responding
    2.2 Willingness to respond
    2.3 Satisfaction in response
3.0 Valuing
    3.1 Acceptance of a value
    3.2 Preference for a value
    3.3 Commitment
4.0 Organization
    4.1 Conceptualization of a value
    4.2 Organization of a value system
5.0 Characterization by a value or value complex
    5.1 Generalized set
    5.2 Characterization [20]

Taking his cue from the taxonomies, Johnson arranged a schema for curriculum. Under that portion classifying learning outcomes, he listed knowledge, techniques, and values as three classes of outcomes. Under values, he listed two subclasses: (1) norms — societal prescriptions and preferences regarding belief and conduct and (2) predilections — individual preferential dispositions (attitudes, interests, appreciations, aversions).[21]

When taxonomies contribute meaningfully to classification, they materially aid the curriculum planner with details of arrangement of curriculum content. They also aid in the development of appraisal instruments. But taxonomies do not help materially with the tasks of selecting values and beliefs to be included in the curriculum. At the moment, two avenues seem available to curriculum planners, and they

[20]David R. Krathwohl, Benjamin S. Bloom, and Bertram B. Masia, *A Taxonomy of Educational Objectives, Handbook II: Affective Domain* (New York: David McKay Company, Inc., 1964), pp. 176-185.

[21]Mauritz Johnson, Jr., "Definitions and Models in Curriculum Theory," *Educational Theory*, 17:138, April, 1967.

have been identified earlier in this chapter. One is to search the recognized school subjects and the scholarly disciplines for value content that reflects decisions made in earlier times. The other is to make judgments about existing values in the general culture ethos of the school and its community. The selection of values is very much a judgmental procedure, and curriculum planners must face up to the task in that light.

IMPLICATIONS FOR CURRICULUM THEORY BUILDING

The implications of values and value theories for theory building in curriculum are not clearly evident. Nevertheless, one has to assume that the acceptance of different value theories would lead to differences in curriculum theories. On the other hand, a case could be made that value theories are also applicable in passing judgment upon curriculum theories. In the absence of clearly stated curriculum theories, it is difficult to test out either assumption scientifically.

To illustrate the difficulties, we might examine where in the work of the curriculum theorist, an assumption of a given value theory might affect his work. One of the most important functions of a value theory is to establish bases, or criteria, for determining what is "good." The intuitive value theorist typically asserts that ideas and principles (values) exist in their own right and that man can become aware of them by the process of intuition. Once aware of them he can use them to guide his own behavior. One who holds pragmatic value theory judges value concepts and principles according to the degree to which they lead to satisfactory consequences. The notion of "goodness" in this case is determined by observation of what people do that brings them satisfaction in life.

Two implications seem to emerge for the curriculum theorist from such variation in value outlook. One implication is for the input information for a curriculum system. What shall be the sources of values to be used as influence upon the work of the curriculum planner? If the theorist chooses the intuitive position, his sources tend to be those that reveal permanent and universal values such as the word of a church, the wisdom of the ancient scholars, or the word of political bodies. If the curriculum theorist chooses the pragmatic position, he is more contextualist; his sources for values are the rules for satisfactory living in the culture in which the school lies. The processes of determining them are observation and experimentation.

A second implication is for the choice of value content to be included in the curriculum. What knowledge about values is to be transmitted to the young through schools? How can that knowledge be most effectively organized as part of a curriculum? What processes for dealing with value problems will the school stress? How shall statements about these processes be arranged in the curriculum so as to lead to the development of effective instructional strategies? Such questions are imperative if curriculum planners are to correct their previous failure to identify the package, or packages, of values the schools are attempting to make an integral part of the educational program. The consequences of the two value theories used here as examples would affect all the questions raised, and they should be apparent from the foregoing discussions. Briefly then, different value theory orientation would influence the work of the curriculum theorist at two points – his treatment of input data for a curriculum system and his treatment of curriculum design.

Value theories and the values derived therefrom can be instrumental in judging the worth of the work of a curriculum theorist as well as in affecting the character of the work. For example, a task for the curriculum theorist is to explain relationships between statements of aims for schooling and the selection of content as a means for achieving the aims. A curriculum planning group may state its aims and select a body of content. In essence, what the group does is to predict that if the content is developed properly through the instructional environment, the aims will be achieved. The theorist must explain this relationship and its ramifications. Many stated aims are value statements exclusively. Others are statements of principle to be used to direct behavior. The latter, in particular, can be used to judge the effectiveness of the theorist's explanation and predictions as well as the predictive operations of the practitioner.

SUMMARY

The implications of values and value theories for curriculum theory have not been explored to the present time in depth. Most, in fact, concede that curriculum planners and other educators have failed to deal with the subject of values adequately for modern schooling. As a consequence, it has been necessary in this chapter for us to explore some of the implications of values and value theories for selected practical aspects of curriculum so that the theoretical implications might be inferred.

At least two dimensions of values have import for a curriculum. The first consists of value concepts and generalizations that may be classified as substantive knowledge. The second is more syntactical; it consists of the processes by which students will learn to deal with value problems and to come to accept values as rules governing their own behavior.

Value theorists have been classified into three groups: the

intuitive, the skeptic, and the pragmatic. Each value position has its unique way of identifying and verifying value judgments. Presumably, each would have a different impact upon the work of the curriculum theorist and the practitioner. We may assume that acceptance of one value theory over others would produce uniqueness in a curriculum theory. We also may assume that the acceptance of one value theory over others would affect uniquely judgments made about curriculum theories.

SUGGESTED READINGS

"A Symposium: What can Philosophy Contribute to Educational Theory?" *Harvard Review*, 28:283-339, Fall, 1958.

Arnstine, Donald G. "Some Problems in Teaching Values," *Educational Theory*, 11:158-167, July, 1961.

Axtelle, George E. "The Humanizing of Knowledge and the Education of Values," *Educational Theory*, 16:101-109, April, 1966.

Bayles, Ernest E. "Are Values Verifiable?" *Educational Theory*, 10:71-77, January, 1960.

Berman, Louise M. (ed.). *The Humanities and the Curriculum*. Washington: Association for Supervision and Curriculum Development, NEA, 1967.

Broudy, Harry S., B. Othanel Smith, and Joe R. Burnett. *Democracy and Excellence in American Secondary Education*. Chicago: Rand McNally and Company, 1964.

Bruner, Jerome S. *On Knowing*. Cambridge: The Belknap Press of Harvard University Press, 1963.

Duncan, Guy. "What Do Americans Value?" *Educational Leadership*, 20:503-506, May, 1963.

Educational Policies Commission. *The Central Purpose of American Education*. Washington: the Commission, 1961.

Goals for Americans. A Report of the President's Commission on National Goals. Englewood Cliffs: Prentice-Hall, Inc., 1960.

Goss, Charles E. "A Critique of the Ethical Aspects of Phenix's Curriculum Theory," *Educational Theory*, 17:40-47, January, 1967.

Hardie, C. D. "The Idea of Value and the Theory of Education," *Educational Theory*, 7:196-199, July, 1957.

Hare, R. M. *The Language of Morals*. Oxford: The Clarendon Press, 1952.

Hook, Sidney. *Education for Modern Man*. New edition. New York: Alfred A. Knopf, 1963.

Hutchins, Robert M. *The Conflict in Education in a Democratic Society*. New York: Harper and Brothers, 1953.

Jarolimek, John (ed.). "Social Studies Education: The Elementary School — Focus on Values," *Social Education*, 31:33-48, January, 1967.

Krathwohl, David R., Benjamin S. Bloom, and Bertram B. Masia. *A Taxonomy of Educational Objectives, Handbook II: Affective Domain*. New York: David McKay Company, Inc., 1964.

O'Connor, D. J. *An Introduction to the Philosophy of Education.* London: Routledge and Kegan Paul, 1957.

Park, Joe. "Values and Education," *Education in Urban Society*, edited by B. J. Chandler, Lindley J. Stiles, and John I. Kitsuse. New York: Dodd Mead and Company, Inc., 1962, pp. 233-248.

"Personal and Social Values," *Educational Leadership*, 21:481-560, May, 1964.

Phenix, Philip H. *Realms of Meaning*. New York: McGraw-Hill Book Company, 1964.

Prior, Moody E. *Science and the Humanities*. Evanston, Ill.: Northwestern University Press, 1962.

Rath, Louis E., Merrill Harmin, and Sidney B. Simon. *Values and Teaching*. Columbus: Charles E. Merrill Books, Inc., 1966.

Smith, B. Othanel, William O. Stanley, and J. Harlan Shores. *Fundamentals of Curriculum Development*. Revised edition. Yonkers -on Hudson: World Book Company, 1957.

Wilhelms, Fred T. "Humanization Via the Curriculum," *Humanizing Education: the Person in the Process*, edited by Robert R. Leeper. Washington: Association for Supervision and Curriculum Development, NEA, 1967, pp. 19-32.

9

EPILOGUE

A lengthy and systematic review for a book of this length would be unduly repetitious. Nonetheless, certain connections between the principal generalizations noted in the preceding chapters and potential next steps in the development of the field of curriculum theory need to be identified. Such is our purpose in this final chapter.

The reader will recall that the purpose of this writing is to update and extend the examination of curriculum theory launched with the publication of the first edition of *Curriculum Theory* in 1961. In the interim, a substantial number of individuals have exhibited interest in curriculum theory through their writing and through their participation in professional conferences and seminars. It is quite apparent that the dialogue about curriculum theory has moved forward despite the fact that very little theoretical research has been done.

Essentially, the same procedures were followed in the research effort for this book as were followed in preparing the first edition. A fresh look was taken at literature describing practices and concepts relating to theory development in behavioral disciplines related to education for cues leading to a discussion of curriculum theory. Next, cues were sought from efforts in theory development within the broad field of education in the belief that curriculum theory must be a sub-theory of educational theory. A third step consisted of noting milestones in the development of ideas about curriculum theory. Finally, an analysis was made of the theoretical issues, problems, and alternatives within various components of curriculum theory.

The principal generalizations reached in the preceding chapters will be discussed under two general headings — those related to the tasks and procedures of theory building and those related to the components peculiar to curriculum theory.

THEORY BUILDING

The fundamental aims of all theorists are to describe, to explain, and to predict. To achieve his aims, the theorist may use any or all of several procedures. He ordinarily accepts the obligation to define his technical terms and use them consistently thereafter. A theorist may develop schemes for classifying knowledge within his field. He may develop models as representations of phenomena and relationships among them that will explain or direct research intended to develop explanation. The conduct of research intended to describe, to reveal causal relationships, or to reveal predictive relationships is a fourth task a theorist may perform. Some theorists will choose to build comprehensive theories; others may choose to work at sub-theory development. All of these are legitimate theory building activities for most theoretical fields, particularly the behavioral sciences. The curriculum theorist works toward the same general aims; he may use all of the procedures employed by any other theorist. The fact that curriculum theorists have not participated in all of these activities in the past may account for their failure to develop systematic curriculum theories up to the present time. That we are currently aware of appropriate theory-building tasks may be interpreted as a prediction that curriculum theorists must come to grips with them in the future if curriculum theory is ever to be developed.

The most serious problem in curriculum theory today is language usage. Variation in meanings associated with technical terms used in curriculum literature tends to reduce communication rather than improve it. Well-defined and consistently-used technical terms are the bases for defining the subject matter of the curriculum field; therefore, they are crucial for the theorist in his work.

A follow-up on the definition of terms is the development of classification schemes for curriculum knowledge. In curriculum work, virtually nothing has been done about classification. In part, this condition may be attributable to the problem of language usage, but it also is due to the fact that few have worked at the tasks of building classification schemes. Among the more obvious implications for future work is the need for descriptive research that will lead to classification schemes. A taxonomy of curriculum knowledge would be a significant contribution.

The paucity of research in the field of curriculum is reported as regularly as research reviews are published; small wonder there is a need for research that will lead to description, explanation, and prediction in curriculum. If curriculum theory is to rise above the level of arm-chair speculation, or the arrangement of taxonomies, those interested in its advancement will have to conduct, or sponsor the conduct of, research intended to reveal causal and predictive relationships among curriculum phenomena. It is only through such systematic research that curriculum theory can become sophisticated and comprehensive theory, and it is primarily through research effort that individuals will develop unique curriculum theories.

Curriculum theorists will use models in at least three ways. One is to use them to represent phenomena that are difficult to represent in other ways or are more clearly represented in model form. A second is to use models to show relationships among phenomena. And a third use is to direct research effort in curriculum.

Virtually no one has worked at the tasks of sub-theory building in curriculum. This condition is a mark of immaturity in curriculum theory. However, we are better able to understand the reluctance of individuals to build sub-theories when we realize the scarcity of well-defined curriculum theories and educational theories. In the future, some theorists will organize curriculum theories so that sub-theories will emerge naturally from them, others will build specific sub-theories, clusters of which may lead to complete curriculum theories. Both approaches should be productive because they have reciprocal effects.

CURRICULUM THEORY COMPONENTS

The components of curriculum theory emerge from a conception of the total field of curriculum. Essentially, the field begins with the concept of *a curriculum* as a necessary instrument in schooling. Under this concept, a curriculum is a document containing an organized set of decisions about what shall be taught in a school, or a group of schools. For the theorist, the technical language surrounding the concept of a curriculum is the language of curriculum design. At the present time, the curriculum theorist searches almost in vain for clear-cut differences in curriculum design. Curriculums are subject, or discipline, centered. In fact, they tend to be organized into separate documents by subject. So much discussion has occurred about the unique structures of discrete disciplines and subjects, that individuals recently have been raising questions about the "whole" curriculum. The latter discussion invites inquiry into modes of organizing a curriculum which, in turn, should produce different curriculum designs.

Some system, or systems, must exist for persons to plan a curriculum, to implement it, and to appraise it. We referred to the establishment and maintenance of such a system as curriculum engineering. Curriculum theorists need to be just as concerned with description, explanation, and prediction with regard to curriculum engineering as curriculum design. To do otherwise is to leave out of curriculum theory one of its principal components. This omission is precisely what is done by individuals who state that a curriculum system, or curriculum practices, are not curriculum and cannot be dealt with theoretically. We must recognize that an individual may wish to concentrate on theorizing about curriculum design, but when he does, it is more accurate to say that he is engaged in sub-theory building. It is encouraging that increasing numbers of people are interested in theoretical explanation of curriculum engineering, and we may look forward to a greater variety of explanations as theorists gain more insight into the issues and problems involved. Such important issues as choice of arena, persons to be involved, the organization of those persons, and procedures to be used by them provide the theorists with important work for many years to come. It is very probable that in the future there will be more differences in curriculum theories due to variation within the component of curriculum engineering than to variation within curriculum design.

Although the large components of curriculum theory are curriculum design and curriculum engineering, there are more. The additional components are best illustrated through the way curriculum is treated as a field of study at colleges and universities. Students and their instructors include in their areas of work, in addition to study of curriculum design and curriculum engineering, selected elements of cultural, historical, philosophical, and sociological foundations of education. Nearly all students of education engage in study of foundations, but it is study for the sake of acquiring general background information. In a specific area of education such as curriculum, and particularly from the point of theory building, the situation demands an entirely different approach. Here the curriculum student or researcher is concerned with extrapolating from educational foundations and cognate areas of study of those concepts, skills, or interpretations needed to advance curriculum theory. For example, the curriculum theorist may borrow heavily from psychological theory, organizational behavior theory, or political theory for models to direct his own thinking and research.

If we add to the above the study of research and theory building, we complete a picture of the total scope of the field of curriculum. Together, these components constitute the means for improving the field of curriculum. Much could be said about weaknesses in curriculum research, but the real hope for growth beyond the present status lies in the forthcoming research effort. Expansion of curriculum theory is impossible without major expansion of experimental research.

Finally, values comprise an important component of curriculum. Within the realm of curriculum theory, values are primarily a problem of curriculum design. Two dimensions of values are important in curriculum design — the substantive and the syntactical. The substantive dimension consists of the value concepts and generalizations that curriculum planners deem important to teach to the young. The syntactical dimension consists of the processes associated with solving value problems and accepting values as rules governing one's behavior. In the past, curriculum planners and theorists have tended to ignore values in school curriculums. This condition is intolerable if schools are to have any effect upon the derivation and perpetuation of social and cultural values. Open conflicts between culture groups constitute a vivid testimony to the need for action on the part of all social agencies, particularly the schools.

IMPONDERABLES

We cannot close this discussion without regard for certain imponderable circumstances that may affect the work of the curriculum theorist. One may speculate that the potential change to be made in conventional modes of schooling has not yet been made visible. Mass media of communication now make it possible to bring the whole world into the school, and conversely, to take the school into the rest of the world. Such technical devices as the computer have opened up completely new vistas for ideas about individualizing instruction. Present schemes are only in their infancy. One can only guess about how technical progress in providing environments for teaching and learning will affect schooling as we now know it. A great revolution in education began simultaneously with the creation of graded textbooks. Textbooks were designed to solve the major problems of schooling. They contained curriculum material — the subject matter. They provided teachers with instructional guides. Frequently, they contained suggested evaluation procedures. Another great revolution is predictable resulting from modern industry producing unit packages designed to solve the same problems for teachers — curriculum decisions, instructional guides and materials, and appraisal instruments. Video tape, the language laboratory, and the talking typewriter are becoming commonplace in today's schools, and they affect curriculum decision-making. To be sure, more will come along. They portend an interesting future.

Technology will have a tremendous effect upon curriculum decisions in the future, but the decisions still will have to be made. When communities of people establish schools, they have some ends in view. When the ends are clear, content (subject matter) may be chosen that has reasonable hope of being a vehicle for the achievement of the ends. The selected content is one means to the ends; instructional strategy is a second. Instructional strategy is in part dictated by the content. Unless our concept of schooling changes drastically, the ends-means continuum will have to be satisfied. Somewhere in the process of decision-making for schools, someone (individual or group) will have to answer the question of what is to be taught in the schools.

Now more than ever before, curriculum theories are needed to cope with impending change. Those of us interested in the field of curriculum theory must recognize that two courses of action are open to us. One is to leave the situation more or less as it now is. In this case, schools will be bombarded with innovations from many sources, and they will be incorporated into existing practices by trial and error. The second course of action is for curriculum theorists to develop organized rationales that will give direction to any change. In this case, there is greater chance that innovation will be directed and deliberate. In the opinion of the author, the second course of action is the more rational choice, and there is some urgency to the need for more and better curriculum theory development.

Index

A curriculum, 6, 67
A curriculum system, 6
Abel, Theodore, 12, 29
Abramson, David A., 149
Administrative personnel, 136, 136
Administrative theory, 3, 4
Aims as value judgments, 160, 161
Alberty, Elsie J., 105
Alberty, Harold B., 105
Alexander, William M., 105, 143
Altman, Burton E., 147, 148, 153
Ammons, Margarent, 101, 142
Anderson, Don W., 75, 105, 142
Anderson, Vernon E., 142
Appraisal scheme, 84, 85
Arena, 69
Arena choices, 117
Arena for curriculum engineering, 116-118
Arnstine, Donald G., 169
Articulation, 131
Assumption, 24, 26
Autonomy in decision-making, 125
Axiological values, 158
Axtelle, George E., 158, 169

Bales, Robert F., 25, 26, 28
Barriers to implementation, 135
Basic concepts, 22
Basic planning procedures, 128
Bateman, Donald G., 147, 153
Bayles, Ernest, 32, 52, 169
Beauchamp, George A., 58, 61, 75, 79, 80, 95, 105, 122, 134, 142

Beauchamp, Kathryn E., 122, 134, 142
Bellack, Arno., 52, 93
Belth, Marc, 47, 48, 49, 52
Berman, Louise M., 169
Black, Hugh C. 35, 36, 52
Bloom, Benjamin S., 105, 165, 170
Bossing, Nelson L. 79, 142
Braithwaite, Richard B., 5, 6, 29
Brameld, Theodore, 35
Brauner, Charles, 45, 46, 52
Broudy, Harry S., 35, 45, 52, 59, 61, 75, 99, 100, 105, 142, 158, 162, 169
Brownell, John A., 91, 106, 143
Bruner, Jerome S., 40, 41, 42, 52, 91, 92, 105, 169
Buswell, G. T., 78, 79
Butter, J. Donald, 35
Burnett, Hoe R., 52, 59, 61, 75, 99, 100, 105, 142, 158, 162, 169

Categories of goals, 94
Cay, Donald F., 142
Caswell, Hollis L., 124, 125
Chandler, B. J., 75, 157, 170
Chandler, K. A., 53
Characteristics of theories, 16-20
Classification, 15, 23-24, 58, 62, 70, 71, 116
Clements, Millard, 52
Coladarci, Arthur P., 37, 38, 53
Committees, 127
Conant, James B., 2, 29

Concepts in curriculum theory, 5-8
Conner, Forrest E., 142
Constructs, 22
Content-centered approach, 88
Content by definition, 78-81
Content and process, 59, 88-90, 114-115
Contents of a curriculum, 78-85
Cooperative involvement, 122
Correlation, 73
Counseling theory, 3, 4
Course offerings in curriculum, 147
Criteria 129, 130
Curriculum
    as a field of study, 6, 68-69, 145-150
    areas of study in, 145
    defined, 63
    definitions of, 78-81
    meanings, 67
    textbooks and courses, 146-148
    types, 86, 87
Curriculum council, 127, 129
Curriculum design, 61, 63, 64, 77-107
Curriculum designs, 78
Curriculum engineering, 108-144
Curriculum evaluation, 137-139
Curriculum guides, 99
Curriculum implementation, 132-137
Curriculum and instruction, 82, 84, 85
Curriculum, instruction and evaluation, 110, 111
Curriculum research, 148-150
Curriculum and schooling, 83
Curriculum systems 59, 63, 68
Curriculum theory
    components, 174-177
    concepts in, 5-8
    defined, 66
    developments in, 55-76
    ingredients, 65-74
    milestones in, 56-65

in perspective, 3-5
Curriculum theory-building activities, 70-74
Cycle of schooling, 81

Definitions, 21, 67
Definition of terms, 20, 22-23, 70
Definition of curriculum theory, 66
Definitions and theory content, 66-70
Deduction, 24, 26
Description, 13, 15
Descriptive theory, 34, 45, 50
Design, 62, 77-107
Design model, 102, 103
Design and organization of schools, 88
Design and schooling, 81-83
Dewey, John, 34
Dimensions of curriculum design, 77-78
Discipline of education, 47, 48, 49
Discipline organization, 90
Disciplines and curriculum content, 91
Disciplines and their structures, 90-92
District arenas, 124
Document features, 83-85
Doll, Ronald C., 142
Domain of values, 157-159
Downey, Lawrence W., 53
Duncan, Guy, 169
Dungan, James R., 75

Educational theory, 3, 31-54,
Eisner, Elliot W., 75
Elam, Stanley, 105
Ellena, William J., 142
Elliott, David Loucks, 76
Enculturation, 155, 161, 162
Ends-means continuum, 161
Ennis, Robert H., 54, 154
Epilogue, 171-179

Evaluation, 61, 64, 69, 137-139
Evaluation of curriculum design, 138
Evaluation of a curriculum system, 138, 139
Evaluation of predicted outcomes, 138
Evaluation scheme, 101
Evaluation of teacher use of curriculum, 137
Evaluation theory, 3, 4
Evans, N. Dean, 143
Experience, 80, 81
Explanation, 13, 15, 18, 64

Faix, Thomas L., 61, 62, 63,76
Faunce, Roland C., 79, 142
Feedback, 59, 64, 69, 85
Feigl, Herbert, 12, 15, 30
Fisher, Carol Mae, 76
Ford, G. W., 76, 105
Forkner, Hamden L., 97, 106
Form and arrangement, 93-99
Foshay, Arthur W., 80, 105
Foundations, 61
Foundational influences, 150-152
France, 122
Frankena, William K., 158
Frasure, Kenneth, 143
Frymier, Jack R., 64, 65
Functions of organization, 127

Gage, N. L., 44, 53
General terms, 22
Generalizations, 58
Getzels, Jacob, 37, 38, 53
Gilchrist, Robert S., 105, 142
Goals and objectives, 83
Goals and subject matter, 93, 94
Goodlad, John I., 76, 94, 95, 105, 149
Gordon, Ira J. 17, 43, 53
Goss, Charles E., 169
Gowin, D. B., 13, 30, 34, 53
Griffiths, Daniel E., 38, 39, 53

Grouping practices, 135
Gwynn, J. Minor, 142

Hall, Calvin S., 11, 23, 30
Halpin, Andrew W., 37, 38, 40, 53
Harap, Henry, 99, 101, 106
Hardie, C. D., 157, 170
Hare, R. M., 170
Harmin, Merrill, 158, 170
Havighurst, Robert J., 126, 135
Heath, Robert W., 105
Herrick, Theral T., 76
Herrick, Virgil, 56
Heusner, Henry C., 134
Hinely, Reginald T., 75
Homans, George, 20, 23, 30
Hook, Sidney, 160, 170
Hopkins, L. T., 79
Horizontal articulation, 131
Huebner, Dwayne, 106, 153
Hughes, Philip, 106
Hughes, Marie M., 53
Humanistic versus scientific, 159-160
Hutchins, Robert M., 170
Hyman, Ronald T., 52

Idealism, 35, 36
Implementation, 84, 101, 132-137
Imponderables, 177-179
Individual school arenas, 124
Inference, 21, 24, 25, 26
Inference and prediction, 70, 71, 72
Inherent values, 156
Inlow, Gail M., 106, 142, 163
Input, 59, 112, 151,
Input data, 114
Instructional guides, 101
Instructional guide worksheet, 96
Instructional theory, 3, 4, 40-44
Instructional values, 156
Involvement, 69
Involvement and arena, 121
Italy, 122, 133, 134

Jarolimek, John, 170
Johansen, John H., 134, 135, 143
Johnson, Mauritz, Jr., 63, 64, 65, 67, 76, 84, 106, 143, 165

Kaplan, Abraham, 17, 19, 26, 30, 156, 157, 159
Kearney, Nolan C., 106
Kerlinger, Fred N., 12, 13, 15, 10
Kerr, J. F., 153
King, Arthur R., Jr., 91, 106, 143
Kitsuse, John I., 75, 157, 170
Kliebard, Herbert M., 52
Krathwohl, David R., 106, 165, 170
Krug, Edward A., 79, 106
Kuethe, James L. 47, 54

Larson, Richard G., 136
Laws, 11, 12, 19, 58
Lay-citizen involvement, 121
Learning outcomes, 84
Learning sets, 92
Leeper, Robert R., 42, 53, 154
Leese, Joseph, 143
Lindzey, Gardiner, 11, 23, 30
Logan, Frank, 10, 30
Logical organization of subject matter, 86

Maccia, Elizabeth S., 49, 52, 62, 63
Maccia, George S., 49, 53
Macdonald, James B., 41, 42, 53, 59, 61, 64, 75, 76, 105, 142, 149, 154
McKim, Margaret G., 97, 106
McMurray, Foster, 35
McNally, Harold J. 143
Masia, Bertram B., 165, 170
Mason, Robert E., 54
Marx, Melvin, H., 30
May, Frank B., 75, 105, 142
Merritt, Eleanor, 99, 101, 106
Miel, Alive M., 79, 80

Milestones in curriculum theory, 56-65
Miller, James G., 30
Models, 21, 26-27, 59, 70, 73
Models of a curriculum system, 113
Moral education, 158
Mouly, George J., 21, 22, 30
Multiple arenas, 122, 125

National arena, 122
National curriculum, 122
Nault, William H., 134
Neagley, Ross L., 143
Newsome, George L., Jr., 33, 53, 54
Nominal definitions, 22
Norms, 162, 165

O'Connor, D. J., 11, 13, 27, 30, 54, 162, 170
Oliver, Albert I., 143
Olmstead, David, 10, 30
Operational construct, 22
Operational definitions, 22
Organization and procedures for curriculum planning, 125, 132
Organizational patterns, 86-88
Organizing centers, 95
Organizing elements, 95
Organizing an instructional guide, 85-99
Output, 59, 63, 68, 112

Page, Ellis B., 54
Paradigm, 39, 40
Park, Joe, 157, 170
Parker, J. Cecil, 89, 106, 154
Parsons, Howard L., 76
Parsons, Talcott, 9, 10, 30
Passow, A. Harry, 97, 106, 143
Perkinson, Henry J., 54
Persistent life situations, 97, 98

Personnel for curriculum planning, 118
Personnel organization, 126, 127
Phases of planning, 128, 129, 130
Phenix, Philip H. 91, 106, 163, 170
Philosophy and curriculum theory, 58
Planning procedures, 125, 126, 127, 128, 129, 130, 131
Planning techniques, 69
Postulates, 26
Pragmatism, 35, 36
Prediction, 12, 13, 15, 18, 21, 24-26, 58, 73
Prescriptive theory, 34, 45, 50
Prior, Moody E., 30, 159, 170
Primitive terms, 17
Process-centered approach, 88
Professional involvement, 124
Programed materials, 92
Psychological organization of subject matter, 86
Psychological values, 158
Pugno, Lawrence, 76, 105

Ragan, William B., 79, 106, 143
Raths, Louis E., 158, 170
Realism, 35, 36
Reconstructionism, 35
Representative involvement, 119
Research 24, 26, 61
Robinson, Helen R., 154
Rose, Arnold M., 11, 30
Rubin, Louis F., 89, 106, 154
Rugg, Harold, 56, 76

Saylor, J. Galen, 143
Schema for curriculum, 63
Schooling, 59, 60, 64, 81, 85
Schwab, Joseph J., 90
Science and humanities, 159
Science and theory, 2
Scobey, Mary-Margaret, 143
Selecting value content, 162-164
Selection and involvement of people, 118-125

Sequence, 91
Shils, Edward A., 30
Shores, J. Harlan, 76, 79, 106, 143, 155, 156, 162, 170
Simon, Sidney, B., 158, 170
Skinner, B. F., 54
Smith, B. Othanel, 54, 58, 59, 61, 75, 76, 79, 99, 100, 105, 106, 142, 143, 154, 155, 156, 158, 162, 169, 170
Smith, Frank L., Jr., 52
Sowards, G. Wesley, 143
Spears, William D., 30
Specialized personnel, 118, 119
Stanley, William O., 76, 79, 106, 143, 155, 156, 162, 170
Statements, 17-20
States as arenas, 123
Stating behavioral objectives, 164-166
Status of curriculum research, 148, 149
Stiles, Lindley J., 75, 157, 170
Strategies, 82
Stratemeyer, Florence B., 97, 106, 143
Structural-functional analysis, 61, 62
Structures of disciplines, 90-92
Study of education, 48, 49
Subject matter, 61, 85, 86, 94
Subjects as value choices, 163
Substantive structures, 90, 91
Sub-theory building, 70, 73
Sub-theory formation, 21, 27-28
Syntatical structures, 90, 91
System interactions, 111
System maintenance, 112
Systems of schooling, 109-112

Taba, Hilda, 107, 131, 144
Talmage, Harriet, 129
Taxonomy, 23, 164, 165
Taylor, Philip H., 107
Teacher commitment, 133
Teacher involvement, 134
Technical terms, 16, 58, 67

Terms
basic, 16
descriptive, 16
technical, 16-17
theoretical, 17, 22
Textbooks in curriculum, 146-148
Thelen, Herbert A., 54
Theoretical terms, 17,22
Theoretical issues in curriculum
engineering, 116-139
Theorizing activities, 20-28
Theory
building, 9-30, 61, 172-174
defined, 10-13
in education, 2, 31-54
functions, 13-16
microcosm, 3, 4
of instruction, 34, 40-44
and philosophy, 34-37
and practice, 1, 32-34
in school administration, 37-40
Total involvement, 120
Toulmin, Stephen, 30
Traditions in American education,
45-46
Travers, Robert M. W., 12, 30,32
Trends in practice, 99-101
Training of personnel, 129
Tyler, Ralph, 95, 107, 143
Types of curriculum theory, 62
Types of curriculum books, 146

Urban districts as arenas, 123
Unruh, Glenys G., 107

Value content, 167
Value implications for curriculum
theory building, 166-168
Value input, 167
Value interpretations, 156-160
Value objectives, 164, 165
Value positions, 157
Value theory, 157. 166
Values, 58, 59, 62
in the curriculum, 160-166

in curriculum theory, 155-170
as principles, 160
Venable, Tom C., 154
Vertical articulation, 131

Walton, John, 47, 54
Wagner, Guy, 79
Wiles, Kimball, 144
Wilhelms, Fred T., 170
Wootton, Lutian R., 147, 154
Writing procedures, 130, 131